dollars &
sense

dollars &
sense

a mom's guide to
money matters

Cynthia Sumner

Revell
Grand Rapids, Michigan

Published by Fleming H. Revell
a division of Baker Publishing Group
P.O. Box 6287, Grand Rapids, MI 49516-6287

Printed in the United States of America

Library of Congress Cataloging-in-Publication Data
Sumner, Cynthia W.
    Dollars & sense : a mom's guide to money matters / Cynthia Sumner.
       p.   cm.
    Includes bibliographical references.
    ISBN 0-8007-3061-5 (pbk.)
    1. Finance, Personal—Handbooks, manuals, etc. I. Title: Dollars and sense.
II. Title.
HG179.S857 2005
332.024—dc22   2005003840

Published in association with the literary agency of Alive Communications, Inc., 7680 Goddard Street, Suite 200, Colorado Springs, Colorado 80920.

To my husband, John,
who has steadfastly guided us toward
a secure financial future,
even when I wanted to go shopping instead

contents

introduction

Master of business administration. My husband and I have a matching set of those diplomas on the wall. We also have about eighteen years of combined experience in the banking business. You would think that we would be the last family to find ourselves in financial difficulty, right? Wrong! How could a couple so eminently qualified to help others manage their money make a train wreck of their own finances? Through the same series of financial setbacks that many families experience today.

A job loss due to corporate downsizing led my husband to take a position with lots of potential but at an initial salary of one-third his previous income. We moved to an area with a lower cost of living, and I tried to cut corners everywhere I could, but as the first year in our new home came to a close, we found ourselves with over $5,000 in credit card debt. Divine intervention was required to get us out of the financial hole we had dug for ourselves. I

received my first book contract and royalty advance just as
our minimum monthly payments threatened to overwhelm
us. Even then, I might have been tempted to rely exclusively
on God's grace to get me out of financial scrapes, except for
some wise words that curiously stayed with me.

A speaker at an annual MOPS International Convention,
Mary Hunt, talked about how excessive debt steals your
financial future—any financial windfalls, like bonuses or
payments for writing a book, are used to satisfy your creditors. Was I thankful for the unexpected income that got
us out of our financial jam? Definitely. Was this the way I
would have preferred to spend my first real paycheck as an
author? Absolutely not. Having to hand my hard-earned
money over to my credit card company was depressing to
say the least, but it pointed out to me, in a very tangible
way, that it was time to make some changes.

My husband and I were skilled at talking the talk, financially speaking, but we needed to start walking the walk by
putting basic money management principles into practice.
What was our first step—to balance our checkbook, set a
budget, organize a garage sale? No. We began by examining the place material things had in our family, their level
of importance, and the role belongings should play in our
approach to life. As one of our founding fathers, Benjamin
Franklin, wrote:

> Money never made a man happy, nor will it. There is noth-
> ing in its nature to produce happiness. The more a man
> has, the more he wants. Instead of its filling a vacuum, it

makes one. If it satisfies one want, it doubles and trebles that want another way. That was a true proverb of the wise man, rely upon it; "Better is little with the fear of the Lord, than great treasure, and trouble therewith."[1]

The Bible offers much wisdom about the "place," and pitfalls, of money. For example, it contains approximately five hundred verses on prayer and more than five hundred verses on faith, but almost two thousand verses on money and possessions—often pointing out how they are a stumbling block to personal and spiritual growth. Scripture reminds us of the importance of trusting our livelihood and security to God and that the distribution of wealth is completely within his providence.

So why should we be concerned with managing our money if the love of it is indeed "the root of all evil" and ultimately beyond our control, to boot? There are several reasons. First, God expects us to be good stewards of whatever gifts he gives us. We are not to become possessed by our possessions but to use them to live as richly as possible. Theologian John Wesley had three rules for managing money:

- Gain all you can.
- Save all you can.
- Give all you can.

One crucial component of living richly is giving from what we have been given, a proposition that is easily overlooked when your mortgage or rent payment is late and you're afraid the check you just wrote at the grocery store will bounce.

Managing your money, as opposed to letting bills, credit card interest, and other assorted financial challenges rule your life, is also important for providing the most secure, stable environment possible for your family. Being proactive in handling your finances *guarantees* that you will be more successful than if you simply wait for notices that your bank account is overdrawn or your credit card has been denied.

If this isn't enough to convince you that it's time to take control of your money, think how great you'll feel when you no longer have the stress of worrying if a creditor will be on the other end of the phone when you answer, and you aren't praying that you can make a deposit before the checks you used to pay bills hit the bank.

It's no secret that families today are struggling to make ends meet. For most, increases in income have not kept up with rising expenses. A decade or so ago, politicians often posed the question, "Are you better off than your parents?" when pointing out the inadequacies, or accomplishments, of an administration's economic policy. I haven't heard that question asked lately, probably because many families can no longer state that their lifestyle exceeds what their parents provided as they were growing up.

What's keeping you from becoming a smart money manager? Are you convinced that you're terrible with numbers? Are you intimidated and confused by financial lingo? Do you think you don't have the time? If getting control of your finances is something you always put off until later, this statistic from the U.S. Department of Agriculture's 2003 Consumer Expenditure Survey brings home the fact that there's no time like the present. The survey found that families today will spend from $130,000 to $260,000 (depending on income level) to raise a child from birth through age seventeen.[2] That's between twenty and forty dollars a day! Money can't buy your child's love, but what about diapers, jars of pureed carrots, and new shoes?

Bookstore shelves hold volumes of publications to help the financial layperson with money management. How is this book different? First, it recognizes that no one system works for everyone. Many moms become discouraged trying to follow the latest "surefire" method to budget or reduce debt, because it feels like they're trying to fit a square peg into a round hole. Each family is unique. That's why you'll find a combination of "expert" advice, practical suggestions, and personal experiences from many moms. By considering a variety of financial solutions, you can pick and choose what will work best for your family. There's even a glossary of common financial terms at the end of the book, with descriptions in plain English, so you can say things like, "We just refinanced with an adjustable-rate mortgage at an initial APR of 5.5 percent"—and really know what you mean!

This book also acknowledges that each of us harbors our own money personality that tends to govern how we handle our finances. The first chapter, "Money 101," examines four general money management types. At the end of most chapters, you'll find a section called "Mom's Money Makeovers" with practical suggestions for ways each of the four money personalities can implement the information and suggestions presented. If you identify closely with one of the money personalities, be sure to read the additional tips under that description, but don't stop there! It can be difficult to find what best applies to each individual family, so browse through all the suggestions at least once to see what fits.

Practicing good money management will not necessarily make you wealthy. You may still, from time to time, run out of money on Wednesday with the next paycheck expected on Friday. But knowing where you are financially is empowering, because then you can make informed choices. An ad for Citibank put it this way: "In the end it is not the one who has the most toys who wins, but the one who learns to live well." My hope is that, in reading this book, you will overcome many of the financial obstacles that prevent you from living well, not so that you can buy more toys, but so that you can focus on what truly matters in life. With that goal in mind, let's get started!

money 101   1

Most of us have *something* that keeps us from addressing
our finances. Often there is a fear we must face, one that
may have originated in childhood or evolved over time. "It
will be too hard." "It will take up too much time." "I will try
and fail." "Finding out where I stand will be too depressing." "If I spend time examining my financial situation,
then I'll have to do something about it." How much easier
it is to live in the land of make-believe, where as long as
you have checks in your checkbook, you still have money
in your checking account! There, ignorance can truly be
bliss—for a while.

Author Peg Bracken wrote, "I believe that one's basic
financial attitudes are—like a tendency toward fat knees—
probably formed *in utero*, or, at the very latest, *in cribbo*."[1] My
own distaste for facing financial realities really did begin in
childhood. My father worked hard to provide a comfortable

life for us, and both of my parents, born right after the Great Depression, were very careful with money. *What's so distasteful about that?* you may be wondering. Unfortunately, I was the kind of headstrong, self-absorbed youngster who took exception to being given limits. While outwardly accepting my parents' statements of, "We don't have enough money for that," inwardly I thought, *When I start making my own money, there will always be enough.* After my husband and I had children and I stopped working, I got used to spending without thinking about it, so that I wouldn't have to tell myself, *We don't have enough money for that.* Thank goodness the sound money management principles my parents modeled for me finally kicked in before I accumulated more debt than we could ever pay off!

Attitudes about finances, good and bad, are easily transferred from one generation to the next. The problem is that children filter their perceptions through a limited set of experiences and sometimes come up with inaccurate assumptions of their own. I recently realized that I had unintentionally conveyed my new, money-saver mind-set to my daughter, and not in a positive manner. Last summer she attended her first "stay away" camp. Each day I repeatedly checked the answering machine and waited on pins and needles for a phone call saying she was lonely, or she wanted me to come pick her up, or just that she was having a great time! My daughter didn't call once during the four nights (and five days, but who's counting) that she was gone. When I picked her up, I told her that I kept thinking I might get a phone call, to which she replied,

"I was afraid to call collect in case you didn't want me to spend the money." Oops. Obviously she had been listening to my occasional statements of, "We can't afford that right now." I had to stop and assure her that any collect phone call from a family member would be welcomed and immediately accepted.

It's worth the time to give some thought to your own attitudes about money and how they came to you. Was the parent who spoiled you a big spender, so you make yourself feel better by buying things? Can you trace an obsession with saving every penny to arguments about money from your childhood? Did you grow up surrounded by friends who felt that money was not all that important? The following money attitudes quiz will help bring your current feelings about money matters into focus—even if you can't pinpoint factors from your own financial history that contributed to those feelings. There are no right or wrong answers, so be truthful with yourself. Keep a record of your responses, because you'll want to refer to them when we talk about money management personality profiles next.

Money Attitudes Quiz

1. When every paycheck comes in, I:
    a. put it into savings and take out just the minimum I think we'll need until the next pay period.
    b. pay any new bills that have come in; place a set amount into separate accounts for things like a

new car, a college-education fund, or retirement; and still have some left over for normal weekly expenses.

c. pay bills that are usually a week or two old.

d. rush out and buy groceries because I ran out of money midweek.

2. When paying bills, I:

    a. pay them off each month as soon as they come in.

    b. use automatic payment whenever possible.

    c. pay only the minimum each time.

    d. make payments late because I forget or don't have the money.

3. If asked the balance in our bank accounts, I would:

    a. know how much is in each, to the penny.

    b. be able to give a close estimate.

    c. know how much is in my checking account, but not the other family accounts.

    d. say, "I have absolutely no idea."

4. Do you know if your family spends more than it earns, and why?

    a. We never spend more than we earn.

    b. We are temporarily spending more than we earn because of a job layoff, medical bills, or whatever, but we are covering the shortfall with savings.

    c. We are spending more than we earn, but we don't know why.

    d. I have no idea.

5. What portion of your income do you save?

   a. 15 percent.

   b. 5 to 10 percent.

   c. I'm not sure, because we always end up spending our savings for some emergency.

   d. Nothing.

6. My family has a plan for how to spend our money:

   a. that we stick to like it's carved in stone.

   b. that we use as a guideline to follow as closely as possible.

   c. that we never can seem to follow.

   d. Plan? What plan?

7. Scrutinizing my own spending and saving habits makes me feel:

   a. in control.

   b. like I am doing the right thing.

   c. like I am wasting my time.

   d. embarrassed and depressed.

8. When a financial question or money emergency pops up, I:

   a. consult a friend who is a professional in order to make an informed decision.

   b. discuss the situation with my spouse (if I have one) and then go talk to my local banker if necessary.

   c. ask parents or other family members for advice or a loan.

   d. use the preapproved checks that came in with my credit card statement.

9. When making a large purchase, I:
   a. make sure it's a necessity that I replace the item, then pay for the purchase from my savings.
   b. take the money out of a savings account set up to pay for these kinds of items.
   c. pay for the purchase with my credit card or by borrowing the money from my bank.
   d. am filled with buyer's remorse the next day because I know I can't really afford the item.

10. My ideal money situation is:
   a. being in complete control of my finances.
   b. being able to buy some things I want, not just what I need.
   c. feeling like I have enough money to go shopping whenever the urge hits.
   d. winning the megalotto.

Now add up the number of As, Bs, Cs, and Ds you chose. This helps determine which of the four following profiles most closely describes your money management personality. If you picked more As than anything else, you tend to be in the category of a Frugal Family Financier. A larger number of Bs indicates that you are a Capable Currency Manager, Cs an Ambitious Breakeven Caretaker, and Ds an Extravagant Home Economist. If your responses are concentrated in a couple of letters, or spread across the board, don't panic. It's entirely possible to have different types of money personalities with respect to the various areas of your finances. Think you know which profile you fall under? Read the following descriptions and see if they hold true.

Frugal Family Financier (FFF). There are two distinctly different reasons why people belong to the FFF club. First, they may be naturally frugal—also affectionately known as thrifty, or even stingy. However, families may also be forced into this category, even if it's not their natural tendency, simply in order to make ends meet. Frugal Family Financiers do everything as cheaply as possible, including clipping coupons and shopping at discount stores. They may or may not own their own home. FFFs usually have only one bank checking and one savings account. Due to their desire to control everything in and out of these accounts, FFFs may not utilize direct payroll deposit or have a debit card. With respect to credit, they may have no credit cards or only one on which they pay the entire balance off each month. Any vacations are taken on a shoestring budget. FFFs hold on to "big ticket" items like cars and major appliances until they can no longer be fixed.

Capable Currency Manager (CCM). CCMs tend to spend everything in their checking accounts, but they won't touch their savings. Friends call them responsible and dependable. They have the discipline to cut back on spending when money is tight, as well as to save in advance for a big purchase. Capable Currency Managers work to save money for their children's college education, for retirement, for big vacations, and for unexpected emergencies. They drive nice, but not new, cars and probably have just one car payment instead of two. CCMs build equity in their homes by paying for home improvements with savings or special bonuses. They have two or three credit cards but really use only one. Credit card balances are kept to a minimum or paid off each month. When they borrow money, Capable Currency Managers shop around to get the best deal possible.

Ambitious Breakeven Caretaker (ABC). The majority of people fall into this category—so much so that you could be considered financially "normal" or "average" if you are an ABC. Ambitious Breakeven Caretakers are hardworking but frustrated because they can't ever seem to get ahead. They aspire to be good money managers, yet they may be plagued with self-doubt about their money management ability. A lack of skills, or sometimes a lack of discipline, keeps them from feeling financially secure. ABCs are able to pay their bills every month and don't have much credit card debt. They know how much money is available, and they spend it! As a result, Ambitious Breakeven Caretakers have trouble saving for the future, or even for big ticket items. Every time ABCs start to save, something comes up.

Extravagant Home Economist (EHE). Is your money already spent before it comes in? EHEs live for today and often live beyond their means. They may be considered indulgent or spendthrifts. As a result, Extravagant Home Economists usually have more credit than they need and use it to excess. They have a hard time passing up all those credit card offers in the mail and over the phone. EHE husbands and wives usually have separate checking accounts. They drive relatively new cars (with a hefty car payment on each) and live in a nicer house than they can truly afford. Vacations are taken on credit or with a loan from a bank or finance company. All this can lead them to request a home equity loan to pay off credit card debt. EHEs often have no retirement savings, except from their employer, and even that may have been borrowed against. Their loans are at higher rates of interest than necessary because they don't shop around.

Recognize anyone in these personality profiles? Understanding your own money management style is the first step toward gaining control over your finances, but you may represent only half of your family's financial equation. For those who are married, combining two separate sets of finances can seem more complicated than a corporate merger. Couples often assume their finances will easily "blend" together, and they ignore the need to reconcile radically different money personalities. Have you ever disagreed with your spouse over whether a purchase was a necessity or an "extra"? Read how some moms responded to this survey question: *What part of dealing with your finances gives you the most difficulty?*

- "Trying to define needs and wants, and staying on the same page as my husband."

- "Approaching finances proactively with my spouse, instead of it always being a crisis response."
- "Agreeing on what's 'worth' spending money on."
- "Sitting down and working with my husband. Having him be a part of our finances."
- "My spouse has a different view of money than I do. I want to save, and he wants to buy things. He never learned how to deal with money because his family was poor."
- "Communication between my husband and me gives us the most difficulty. We have a budget and, for the most part, stick to it. The problem comes in when our discretionary income gets spent twice. It really comes down to the two of us taking the time to really see the plan as our plan, not as his or my plan."

Addressing your and your spouse's unique approaches to money management, first individually and then together, helps bridge the money personality gap (or chasm, for some) and allows you to work together as a team. Unfortunately, discussing finances with your spouse often ranks high on the anxiety scale—second only to the "birds and bees" talk you have with your kids! When my husband and I have "the talk" at our house, it's hard for one, or both, of us *not* to start off feeling territorial and defensive. However, there are things you can do to encourage financial equity and cooperation in your household, and they are not dependent upon who brings home the bacon.

Setting Up Checking Accounts

One of the first challenges couples face when setting up housekeeping is learning to handle their day-to-day finances jointly. And even if you've managed your money together amicably before becoming parents, the arrival of children presents new financial concerns that may require a change. In our case, my husband and I began married life with just one joint checking account, following the pattern of my parents. Being an independent career woman who eventually transitioned to stay-at-home motherhood, I didn't like the feeling of being given an "allowance" in a separate account for my weekly purchases. Somehow it seemed more equitable if all the money were in one big communal pot. This system actually worked well for us until two things happened: my husband took a new job with a serious pay cut, and debit cards became available.

Finances were tight, and with two preschoolers (and then three), we really didn't have time to update our respective checkbooks with each other's transactions every day. My husband and I never really knew how much we had to spend, but that didn't keep us from buying what we needed. Our lack of cooperation, combined with those pesky debit cards, resulted in overspending—and eventually overdrafts. Individually we were responsible money managers; together we spelled financial disaster.

The solution to this problem came from—who else— my girlfriends. One day we took a shopping trip together, and on the drive home, someone brought up the subject of household finances. (Not me; I was way too embarrassed about the state of my checkbook.) I listened quietly as my friends compared their money management systems. By the end of the trip I had decided it was time to "restructure" our bank accounts.

Today my husband and I each have our own checking account. Although both of our names are on each account, we manage them separately. Now I don't overdraw my account when my spouse forgets to write down several days' worth of debit transactions in the checkbook. My hubby doesn't have to worry that we're spending more than we earn, because having the accountability of my own checkbook balance keeps me from buying what I can't afford. By mutual agreement, we never refer to the amount deposited into my account as an allowance. I prefer to think of it as my salary for the important role I play in maintaining the "business" of our family.

Wondering if it's time to "restructure" the way you handle your bank accounts? Let's take a look at the pros and cons of three possibilities for family checking accounts.

One account. A couple has the most control over finances with one checking account. All of your money is in one place, so it's easier for you both to see how much is being spent and on what. You may also save on fees with fewer accounts. On the negative side, as my husband and I found, busy couples with kids may not have enough time to consistently keep checkbooks up-to-date. Some families may choose to use just one checkbook, which is fine as long as the person *without* the checkbook doesn't resort to using a credit card on a regular basis! A final "con" to this method: the partner who contributes less to the family's income may feel like he or she has no money of his or her own to spend, especially if that partner doesn't work outside the home.

Two accounts. When each partner has a separate checking account, both can be responsible for their own money and how to spend it. Of course, two accounts make it more challenging to keep track of how much is spent, as a family, in various expense categories. You will also have to negotiate, and renegotiate, how to divide the family's monthly income between the accounts and who will pay for what. A stay-at-home mom can be placed in the uncomfortable position of feeling like a child who receives an allowance—especially if she has to ask for more money to cover unexpected expenses.

Having experienced this unsettling sort of time travel, the only long-term solution my husband and I have found is communication of our financial needs and an honest sharing of our feelings about family money matters. Ever since I explained my distress at having to sheepishly ask for extra cash to cover an occasional unexpected bill, my hubby makes every effort *not* to point the finger or make me feel guilty. This positive reinforcement contributes to family harmony by removing the tendency to engage in a financial "turf war."

Three accounts. If you are a two-income family and want to preserve some financial autonomy, both partners can contribute a portion of their paychecks to a joint "household account" to be used for paying all the joint monthly bills (like mortgage or rent payments, insurance, utilities, car payments, and groceries). To determine how much each partner should put in, first estimate your joint monthly expenses. Then calculate the percentage of total income you and your spouse each bring home in a pay period, and apply that percentage to the amount of money you'll need in your joint household account. Here's an example: You work part-time and receive a paycheck of $110 per week. Your husband brings home $660 per week. Your total weekly family income is $770, of which you contribute 14 percent ($110 divided by $770, then multiplied by 100 to get the percentage) and your spouse contributes 86 percent ($660 divided by $770 multiplied by 100). You estimate that total weekly bills come to $500. If you deposit $70 ($500 times 14 percent) of every paycheck into the joint household account, and your hubby deposits $430 ($500 times 86 percent), you each will be contributing to your family's expenses in the same proportion as the income you earn. Obviously this is not an *equal* sharing of resources, but many couples feel it is an *equitable* one.

Paying Bills

Another financial task couples wrestle with is bill paying. Who actually pays the bills is irrelevant as long as they are paid on time and *both* parties know approximately how much is being spent on monthly expenses and on "extras." Often the person who does not write the checks uses that fact as an excuse to be uninformed about the family's finances, perhaps because he or she doesn't feel comfortable with money issues. Unequal responsibility in managing money can cause an unfair amount of stress for the bill payer, as this mom relates:

> I am a stay-at-home mom, and I'm responsible for the finances. My husband literally leaves it all up to me. I hate the responsibility (especially when there is NEVER enough money), but I realize if I don't do it, it won't get done. My husband is wonderful in most other areas, but this one is really hard for me to handle. I feel like I'm always "telling" him what he can or can't do. I hate that he comes to me and asks if he can buy something. I usually have to say it's not something we need, so he probably shouldn't. Or he gets something we don't really need, and I have to decide whether to just let it go and try to figure out how to make everything work out, or to tell him he's GOT to stop doing that!

It's not unusual for one spouse to play the primary role in managing finances, and this job typically falls on the woman. Still, it is critical that both partners are involved and aware. Money-related tasks should be divided up just like household chores. To ensure that you both are knowledgeable about your family's income and expenses, take turns paying the bills, or sit down and pay them together. In our household we have a flexible agreement about who pays what, so my hubby and I both write checks. Although he pays the mortgage and utilities, I usually open the bills when they come in so I stay on top of these expenses. We keep unpaid bills and paid receipts in a central location so either of us can look through them at any time. There is no one right way to share bill-paying responsibilities; just make sure that you both understand who handles what so that payments aren't missed.

Couples should also have a periodic money "summit." Get together to talk objectively about your finances at least every six months; once a month or quarter would be even better. Schedule these meetings when you can give the subject, and each other, your full attention—in other words, not while driving or with kids chasing each other around the room. Try to keep these money summits emotion free—avoid playing the blame game, or you'll end up feeling like money adversaries instead of financial partners. Keep money the main topic. Don't allow disagreements about other things, like your in-laws, to derail your conversation. Good communication is key in order for you to share financial responsibility and avoid stressful money squabbles.

Mom's Money Makeovers

All money personalities should take the money attitudes quiz and encourage their partners to do the same. Consider your quiz responses when answering the following questions:

• Does your financial lifestyle reflect your attitudes about money? If not, where do they differ?

- If you and your spouse have conflicting money management personalities, what are the major areas of disagreement?

Begin reconciling financial differences by being respectful of your partner instead of judgmental. As with many other aspects of relationships, opposites often attract. It may be that the free-spending attitude you loved during courtship is the same behavior that's putting you in debt now. Your money personalities haven't changed, but your circumstances have.

Frugal Family Financiers and Capable Currency Managers. If you fall under one of these personality profiles, congratulations! You have made a commitment to financial responsibility. However, you may be having trouble pursuing that commitment for two reasons: you are an FFF or CCM while your partner is an Extravagant Home Economist (this is otherwise known as a spender-saver conflict), or you both are FFFs or CCMs but your partner's need to control the finances results in information about, responsibility for, and ownership of the family's money being unfairly concentrated under his power.

If you have conflicting money personalities, look for recurring patterns and issues, and discuss together what attitudes and feelings about money are driving those behaviors. Brainstorm about ways to avoid falling into the same patterns in the future. Talking openly about money matters is the only way to keep these differences from growing and festering. Couples with control issues need to understand that they both are responsible for managing the family's money. Sharing information and decision making increases your chances of financial success and puts your relationship on solid ground.

Ambitious Breakeven Caretakers. ABCs can feel very anxious when it's a struggle each week to make ends meet. It may help to realize that most families do not start off feeling financially secure. Particularly with young children in the mix, parents must spend the majority of their disposable income just to meet everyday needs. It's tough not to be able to afford all the things you want, but financial security is a goal families can work toward over time. The notion that money buys happiness is a myth. Studies show that couples with a lot of money argue about finances almost as regularly as those with a little. Don't let the challenges of day-to-day money management derail your attempts to get ahead. If you are "stuck" on what you've done wrong, look again at each mistake as a learning experience. You've eliminated an approach that doesn't work and moved a step closer toward figuring out what does.

Extravagant Home Economists. To gain control over your money, consider consolidating your family's finances into one checking account, one savings account, and one credit card. In this situation it's best not to use a debit card unless you keep the card with your checkbook so that charges can be written down right away, before they're forgotten. If you have not been involved with paying the bills, this is a good time to take your turn. Tell your spouse you'd like to write the checks for at least the next three months to see how much your lifestyle is costing you. He'll probably be more than happy to give you the opportunity.

set financial goals 2

There's a big closet next to my daughter's bedroom that I call our "junk room" (also known as the "black hole"). Every year I make a resolution to clean it out, but now there's so much clutter that I can't figure out how to start. I really have no choice but to begin sorting things at the door and work my way forward. Setting financial goals is like tackling a big project; you choose a starting point—now—and work your way forward.

Do you know what activities are on your calendar for next week? Next month? Three months from now? Planning your financial future can seem like a big first step when all you really want to do is learn how to reconcile your checkbook and *not* have a negative balance at the end of each week. When you're living hand-to-mouth, it's hard to look down the road toward financial goals.

Most of us need an incentive to do something that may be hard or distasteful, like spend less money. Setting realistic goals gives you an incentive to be disciplined about saving money. It's always easier to change your behavior if you have a defined, measurable goal to work toward, especially if you break that goal into smaller parts. Say you want to begin working toward a goal by saving $10 each week. It may be easier to stick to that plan if you realize that $10 is only about three Starbucks Frappuccinos, three packs of cigarettes, two lunches at McDonald's, one medium pizza, or five video rentals.

The process of developing a financial plan can be just as important as the plan itself, because it encourages you to take an objective, in-depth look at your situation. The first step is to write down your goals. Dreaming about the way you'd like to live doesn't cost a thing, so brainstorm about what you want to accomplish financially. Ask yourself what you want to be doing one year from now, five years from now, and ten years from now.

The more specific and measurable you make your goals, the easier they will be to achieve. Also, pursuing your dreams should be an enjoyable process, so try to phrase your goals in the positive rather than the negative. Instead of "I *won't* spend money on anything that's not a necessity," try "I *will* save enough money for the down payment on a house." If you're one half of a couple, write down your goals independently, and then discuss them together to find areas the two of you have in common. When you've identified similar priorities, it's easier to decide how to organize your finances to meet those goals.

Next, put your goals in order, from most important to least, for each time period. Stair-step short-term goals to make it easier to accomplish one or two of them as the year goes by. For example, focus on paying off the credit card balance with the highest interest rate in eight months, then see how much you can reduce the balance on another card by year's end. Small successes like these are the best encouragers to keep you on track.

Most families also intend to pursue longer-term goals, like

- Reducing other debt
- Buying a home or car
- Starting a savings plan that can be for short-term contingencies, long-term retirement, your children's education, or even to give something back to your church or community

How do you choose which need to work toward first, with so many of them competing for your funds? There's only a limited amount of money available at any one time to satisfy your goals, so it's necessary to prioritize. Start by looking at two factors: the importance of the goal and how long before you'd like to achieve it (also known as the "time horizon"). If your family has outgrown its living accommodations and you'd like to move into a new house in two years, the goal of saving for a down payment will probably take precedence over putting money into your children's college fund. Since having more than one bathroom is *very* important to you, and the time until you'd like to move is relatively short, it only makes sense to put all your savings toward that goal, right? Well, yes and no.

Since a new home is a priority for the near future, you will want to channel the *majority* of your savings in that direction. However, it's in looking out to the more distant future that we truly see the importance of setting financial goals as early as possible. Financial procrastination can be costly. The longer you wait to start saving to achieve your goals, the more they will cost you on a monthly basis, as seen in the following chart.

Diagram 1: Monthly Savings Needed to Accumulate $25,000

Years to Save	Monthly Savings at 2 Percent	Monthly Savings at 4 Percent	Monthly Savings at 6 Percent
14	$129.07	$111.25	$95.31
10	$188.37	$169.78	$152.55
6	$327.09	$307.80	$289.32
2	$1,021.84	$1,002.29	$983.02

If your goal is to save $25,000 for your child's college education in fourteen years, you will have to put away $95.31 each month while earning 6 percent on your investment. If you only have ten years until your child starts college, you will have to save $152.55 each month at that same interest (or earnings) rate. Every year you wait translates into more money you will have to save monthly to reach your goal. That's why, when it comes to longer-term goals, the sooner you start, the better off you'll be.

After you've chosen a set of financial goals, it's time to create a plan to help you accomplish them. Outlining a financial plan sounds daunting but is fairly simple for most families. It begins by following John Wesley's second rule for managing money: save all you can. Until you free up some money to work with, it's tough to make progress toward a goal. In the next chapter we'll take a look at getting control of your finances by using the "B" word—budgeting. For now you can begin by starting to save, even if it's only five or ten dollars a week.

Once a year, pull out your list of goals, and have an annual "performance review" to see what progress you've made toward achieving them. If your financial plan is not working the way you'd like, it's time to make some adjustments. Realistically there are only three actions you can take to have more money available:

1. Cut back on the money you spend or increase the amount you make.
2. Push the time horizon to reach your goal further into the future so you'll have the opportunity to put more money away.
3. Decrease the amount of your goal and consider less expensive options.

Choose one of these alternatives, and make the changes necessary to get your dreams and financial realities back in line.

Certified Financial Planners

Many people wonder if they need the services of a financial planner to help them through the goal-setting and investing process, which can feel overwhelming and a bit intimidating. There is a broad range of professionals who assert that they can give financial advice—bankers, life insurance brokers, securities brokers, and independent certified financial planners. Some of these people may steer you toward the products they represent. There are basically two ways financial planners earn their living: through the commissions they earn on products they sell to you, like investments or life insurance, or on a fee basis, which may depend on the value of your investment portfolio.

The type of financial planner who would be willing to work with a young family just starting to set financial goals is usually the commissioned kind, because they can earn some income for the work they do even if their clients don't have a lot of money to invest. Advice from someone who operates on a fee basis will be more independent, but these types of financial planners can require a large initial investment to make use of their services. The Financial Planning Association maintains a website where you can find a certified financial planning professional nearby (www.fpanet.org), or you can simply ask relatives, neighbors, and friends whom they use. Asking them what the best and worst things are about working with their planner can help narrow your list of candidates.

Next, call to schedule some interviews. Make sure you will not be charged for these initial meetings. A good financial planner will ask you lots of questions about your current financial situation and walk you through the goal-setting process. You should come out of an interview with a clear idea of the services the planner will provide and the way in which he or she will be paid. Ask for references, and check them, before making a final decision. You can also check the records of the financial planners in your area with the Better Business Bureau for any complaints.

Insurance

Another part of setting financial goals is providing for your family in the event of an emergency or catastrophic loss. Insurance agents have "rule of thumb" formulas for how much life insurance you should carry and opinions about what kinds of coverage are best for your home and car. However, deciding how much insurance to have really comes down to striking a balance between what you need and what you can afford. For example, most families carry life insurance coverage of three to five times their annual income (if they have any at all), while the recommended amount is six to ten times. Realistically, families facing the choice between making a car payment each month or buying more insurance will opt for the vehicle nine times out of ten.

There are many different kinds of insurance available today. Let's take a brief look at the types of policies most often held by families.

Life. The amount of life insurance you need varies according to several factors, like the number of dependents in the family and their ages, as well as family income level. A stay-at-home mom with three preschool and elementary-age children would need a substantial amount of money to raise the family to adulthood in the event of her spouse's death, whether she entered the workforce or not. That's why insurance companies suggest families carry such a large multiple of their annual income in life insurance—so that money will be available to satisfy your current expenses with enough left over to invest for future needs.

There are two basic types of life insurance policies: term and whole life. Term life policies are in effect for a specific amount of time and only pay upon death. Whole (or permanent) life policies offer both death benefits and a "cash value." The cash value can be compared to an investment that you pay into, which increases in value over time. If needed, you can cash in the policy or borrow against it. You can buy much more coverage for the same amount of money with a term policy because the rates are so much less. The catch is that premiums for term life tend to increase over time. With whole life policies, premiums don't necessarily change, and your coverage stays level or increases.

Since you can get more coverage for less money with a term policy, the standard advice is "buy term and invest the difference." This may hold true if you do invest the difference. But being this disciplined is difficult for many families, so insurance agents often suggest that you utilize a combination of both whole and term life insurance. That way you'll earn something for all the money you've paid out.

Home. If you've bought a home, your mortgage lender has almost certainly required you to have homeowner's insurance sufficient to cover your loan amount. The most complete coverage available, and the most expensive, is for the replacement cost of your house and the replacement cost of the contents. With this type of policy, the insurance company will replace your home and belongings at their current cost versus simply reimbursing you for the *value* of the items, taking into account their age and condition. Say you have a seven-year-old refrigerator that works just fine. With a replacement-cost policy, you could simply go buy a brand-new fridge if yours was destroyed in a kitchen fire. A basic policy on household contents would only send you a check for the depreciated value of a seven-year-old refrigerator, which, you can imagine, would probably not be enough to buy a new one. However, this insurance option can save on premiums.

Our own insurance agent contacts us every three years to perform a review of our coverage. This level of service is beyond what most people receive, now that the majority of insurance policies renew automatically, but it is a good idea for you to review your insurance policies every few years for both coverage and price competitiveness.

Auto. Automobile owners are required by law to have liability insurance on their vehicles, and your lender (if you're still paying for your car) will require you to carry collision insurance up to the value of the car. Maintaining a good driving record and researching rates are two things you can do to keep insurance premiums to a minimum. (No more pedal to the metal!) If your car is at least ten years old, you may want to consider dropping collision insurance coverage and carrying only liability insurance. You'll save money on insurance premiums, which could eventually be used toward putting a larger down payment on your next car.

There are two other points to consider with respect to saving money on insurance. One is that many companies offer "package credits" off both homeowners' and auto insurance rates if you buy both from them (10 percent or more according to our agent). Companies also now decide whether or not to provide you insurance, and at what rate, with "credit scoring," which is based on your payment history, amount of credit outstanding, amount of credit available, and the existence of any judgments or liens against you. The rationale is that people with better credit are more responsible in paying their bills (including insurance premiums) and tend to have fewer claims. Yet another reason to get your finances in order!

Wills

In the busyness of caring for a growing family, moms rarely consider how their kids would manage without them. The idea is unthinkable! How could kids possibly get by without the person who takes care of their every need? Our hearts may shudder at the prospect, but our heads know that we want the very best for our families, even if we're not there to provide it. Preparing a will is the only real way to choose your children's guardian and have your assets distributed as you would like in the event of your death.

What happens if you die without a will varies according to the law of the state where you live. In my home state of Illinois, property does not automatically go to the surviving spouse. Instead, it is divided between the spouse and any children. This can result in additional expenses if you have to dispose of some jointly owned property, like selling the family home.

A will can allow you to assign two kinds of guardians over your children. A "guardian of the person" makes decisions about where the minor child lives, what church he or she attends, and his or her social activities. However, many of us know people whom we think would do a good job of raising our children but not such a good job of handling their money, and vice versa. A separate "guardian of the estate" can also be chosen to handle your children's money matters. Other devices can be written into a will, like invoking the Uniform Transfers to Minors Act (see glossary), to protect your children from the unscrupulous use of their assets by others.

If you decide to have an attorney prepare your will, what information should you get together before your appointment? First discuss with your spouse the fundamental question: do you want to provide for your kids equally or based on need? This is particularly important if one of your children has special needs that require greater expenses for his or her care. Other information to bring with you includes the names and birth dates of your children and a list of family assets and liabilities. Your lawyer can include a clause for later-born or adopted children so the will doesn't have to be changed as you add to your family. Attorneys can prepare wills that are good in almost every state, but if you move, it's a good idea to take your will to a local attorney for review.

Several software companies have programs available for you to use to prepare your own will. In most states these basic wills are acceptable. However, such software generally does not allow for the inclusion of finer details like dual guardianship, uniform transfers to minors, and family trusts, among others. Carefully consider your family's situation and future needs when deciding who should prepare your will.

Mom's Money Makeovers

The process of setting financial goals is for everyone, regardless of how much or how little you have. Part of developing a financial plan involves thinking about contingencies in the event of various happenings. Don't feel like you have to be an expert in every area of planning. Take advantage of the knowledge of professionals in the areas where you lack experience.

Frugal Family Financiers. Make sure you aren't saving money at the expense of protecting your family. Even if you are an excellent saver, it's unlikely that you've saved enough to put your children through college or to fund your retirement in the event of the death of the primary breadwinner. Paying for the preparation of a will and for insurance is not a waste of money. If you haven't taken care of these important safeguards, just do it!

Capable Currency Managers. You're more likely to have taken care of all aspects of setting financial goals, but have you kept things up-to-date? It may be time to revise your list of goals to reflect any life changes you've experienced. Reread your will, and check with your insurance agents to make sure you have as much coverage as you'd like.

Ambitious Breakeven Caretakers. If you've thought about financial planning but never gotten started, the time is now. Sit down and start by writing out your financial goals. Make a commitment to get yourself on track by putting together a list of telephone numbers for insurance agents, attorneys, and financial planners if you like. Call at least one person on the list each day, or make one appointment each week, until you've found professionals with whom you feel comfortable.

Extravagant Home Economists. The state of your finances may make it impossible for you to pay for the services of a financial planner or to buy more insurance at this time. If your situation is desperate, read on into the next chapter to find out how to get control of your finances and free up enough money to take steps toward your financial goals.

get control of
your finances 3

When my kids were toddlers, they would occasionally lose control and throw a tantrum. Shocking as this behavior was the first few times, these outbursts rarely came on out of the blue. Usually there were small actions that, taken individually, didn't amount to much. When they came one right after the other, however, these behaviors had a snowball effect, eventually leading to a big crash. If I caught my children before that behavioral snowball started gaining momentum, we often could work together to smooth out the situation and avoid the crash. Once things went too far, it was virtually impossible to hold off a full-blown tantrum.

Getting control of your finances is a lot like dealing with a child in the terrible twos. The earlier you catch missteps, like overdrawn checking accounts and too many charges on credit cards, the easier it is to solve the problem and avoid a money disaster. But unlike dealing with a child's tantrum, the best course of action for those in a financial crash is *not* to ignore the whole thing and hope it will be over soon. You have to take the initiative.

Balancing Your Checkbook

The first step to getting control is finding out where you are financially *right now*, and that means doing something approximately half of us don't do—balancing your checkbook. Keeping up with the amount of money in your checking account serves two main purposes:

1. Holding your spending in check by showing how much money you have (or don't have).
2. Saving on bank fees from overdrafts or too-low account balances.

If you have never balanced your checkbook before, dealing with all those numbers can seem scary. It may help to remember that you deal with numbers every day: scoops of formula and ounces of water, price per pound of meat at the grocery, and amounts of ingredients for a recipe. In fact, balancing your checkbook can be just like following a recipe. Knowing how much money you have available is the first step in making good choices about how much you spend, so grab your checkbook register (where you record the checks you've written) and your current bank statement, and try one of these suggestions to get yourself in balance.

Quick-Fix Recipe

When you get ready to make a recipe, the first thing to do is check the list of ingredients against what you have on hand in order to figure out what is missing. If you want a quick fix for your current checking account, begin writing down all checks, deposits, and other debits (ATM or debit card transactions and automatic deductions) right away. When the next bank statement arrives, see what transactions you have in your checkbook register that are missing from your bank statement, and vice versa. To ensure the entries on your bank statement and in your checkbook register match, a good financial cook will make time for a BAD SOB. (Not a result of a lower-than-expected cash balance!) Try this method to reconcile your checkbook balance to the statement by looking through the latest month's transactions:

Bank Balance	use bank statement ending balance, not the beginning
+ **A**dd **D**eposits	appearing in your checkbook register but not appearing on the statement
– **S**ubtract **O**ustanding checks	those you've written but not on the statement
= **B**alance	should equal your checkbook balance on the same closing date

Let's take a look at an example using the transactions in a (mostly) fictitious checkbook register and bank statement. Diagram 2 is a portion of a bank statement for the month of May, and a checkbook register page from May is Diagram 3. In the top right-hand corner of the bank statement, you'll see two numbers under "Balance." The

Diagram 2: Bank Statement

```
Your Account Type Is:   Regular Account
Checking Summary............Account        Pieces  59        Balance
Previous Statement Balance (04/30/04)                         756.41
        12 Deposits / Credits........  4,148.87
           Interest Paid.............
        47 Checks / Debits...........  3,756.68
           Statement Balance (05/28/04)                     1,148.60
------------------------------------------------------------
Deposits / Credits.......... Account
                05/04/04   Customer Deposit          42.00
                05/04/04   Customer Deposit         387.00
                05/07/04   Customer Deposit         340.00
                05/12/04   Customer Deposit         100.00
                05/12/04   Customer Deposit         150.00
                05/14/04   Customer Deposit         340.00
                05/20/04   Customer Deposit         106.00
                05/24/04   Customer Deposit         340.00

------------------------------------------------------------
Checks / Debits............. Account

05/03*  3370          50.00  Customer Check
05/06*  3380          17.75  Customer Check
05/06*  3392          50.00  Customer Check
05/05*  3394         115.00  Customer Check
05/03*  3396          18.00  Customer Check
05/04   3397         135.08  Customer Check
05/27   3398          50.00  Customer Check
05/04   3399          50.00  Customer Check
05/04*  3402          42.08  Customer Check
05/05   3403          90.00  Customer Check
05/05   3404         178.48  Customer Check
05/11   3405          16.16  Customer Check
05/24   3406         220.00  Customer Check
05/21   3407          42.50  Customer Check
05/06   3408          11.26  Customer Check
05/07   3409          13.78  Customer Check
05/10   3410          93.34  Customer Check
05/13   3411          42.25  Customer Check
05/12   3412          10.94  Customer Check
05/12   3413          20.00  Customer Check
05/21   3414          50.00  Customer Check
05/11   3415           7.40  Customer Check
05/12   3416           3.96  Customer Check
05/13   3417          20.03  Customer Check
05/12   3418          54.10  Customer Check
05/14*  3421         133.25  Customer Check
05/17   3422          11.96  Customer Check
05/17   3423          68.08  Customer Check
05/17   3424          62.22  Customer Check
05/19   3425          22.81  Customer Check
05/19   3426          28.64  Customer Check
05/17   3427           9.00  Customer Check
05/17   3428          60.00  Customer Check
05/21   3429          38.55  Customer Check
05/21   3430           3.95  Customer Check
05/25*  3432          49.34  Customer Check
```

Diagram 3: Checkbook Register

Item Number	Date	Transaction Description	T	Check or Debit (−) Amount	Deposit or Credit (+) Amount	Balance Fwd.		
8425	5/14	Main Street gift	✓	22 81				
8426	5/14	Berkott's groceries	✓	28 64				
8427	5/17	Market Day cookie dough	✓	9 00				
8428	5/17	Dr. Carter check-up	✓	60 00				
8429	5/18	Berkott's groceries	✓	38 55				
8430	5/19	Postmaster	✓	3 95				

——	5/19	Deposit — Book sales	✓		106 00			
8431	5/19	IMH medical co-pay	O	20 00				
——	5/21	Deposit — money from John	✓		340 00			
8432	5/20	Factory Card Outlet graduation supplies	✓	49 84				
8433	5/20	Sam's groceries	O	117 14				
8434	5/22	Kohl's clothes	O	115 00		896 46		

first one is the beginning balance (also the balance as of the end of the previous statement). Below that is the ending balance as of the date of the statement, which is the end of May. That's the first number for our BAD SOB reconciliation.

Now take a look at the checkbook register page. Imagine that this person went on vacation after writing the last check shown in the register, so the checkbook register entries for May end on May 22. You'll notice that the last two deposits on the bank statement appear in the checkbook register, so the amount of deposits in the register but not appearing on the statement equal zero. I've recorded that fact by placing a check in the column with a check mark in the heading. I like to make it obvious that I've written some checks that do not appear on the statement by drawing a big "O" in this same column. That's why you'll see an "O" next to the amount for check numbers 3431, 3433, and 3434. If you total the amounts of these three checks, the sum will be $252.14, which is the third number we need. Now let's put our numbers into the reconciliation:

$1,148.60 (**B**ank balance)
+   0.00 (**A**dd **D**eposits outstanding)
-   252.14 (**S**ubtract **O**utstanding checks)
= $896.46 (**B**alance)

This adjusted bank balance equals the balance as of the end of the month in the checkbook register.

After completing this exercise with your own bank statement and checkbook register, you may indeed give a bad sob, but you'll be on your way to reaching a financial starting point. If your checkbook and bank statement balance, congratulations! However, if you are new to reconciling and only looked at the most recent transactions, you may not have a completely accurate checkbook balance. The majority of checks and other transactions come through the bank within a month; however, there are occasional "straggler" checks that can show up later. After reconciling your account for a couple of months, you may want to make a permanent adjustment to your checkbook balance so it will equal future statements. For those who are still scratching their heads over this explanation, your bank statement usually has a form on the back of the page to help you reconcile your bank balance to your checkbook balance; it looks something like the chart on the following page.

Cooking from Scratch

Stop writing checks for a month or two, and pay for everything you can with cash. This should be enough time for all the checks you've written in the past (your outstanding checks) to clear. Then call the bank, or check online, and find out your current balance. Use this number as your balance to start from scratch in the check register. Be sure to balance your checkbook every month from now on.

Making Substitutions

The surest way to have a balanced checkbook is to substitute a new account for your old one. Open another account,

Diagram 4: Balancing Your Bank Statement

Checks Outstanding—Not Charged to Account

No.	$	
TOTAL	$	

Bank Balance Shown on
This Statement
$_____

ADD +
Deposits Not Shown on
This Statement (If Any)
$_____
$_____
$_____

TOTAL $_____

SUBTRACT –
Checks Outstanding
(If Any)
$_____

BALANCE $_____
Should agree with your
checkbook balance after
deducting service charge
(if any) shown on this
statement.

but make sure you leave enough money in the old account to cover checks that you've written (estimate how much). After a month, close out your original account, and deposit any remaining money in the new account.

The difficulty here is having sufficient balances in both accounts to avoid any extra service charges. Many moms don't have that kind of cash lying around. If automatic deposits or withdrawals are made to or from the old account, you also will have to contact those companies and give them your new account information.

Once you have an accurate, reliable balance, keep it up-to-date by following these additional steps:

1. Make sure you always record every transaction that affects your checking account.
2. Use checks with carbon copies if you have trouble remembering to record them in your checkbook register. However, this won't help you with other transactions, like ATM withdrawals.
3. Every month when you receive a new bank statement, pull out your checkbook register, and verify your balance against the bank's. Banks make mistakes on occasion, but they are not required to correct them if the errors are reported more than sixty days after you receive the statement.
4. If the two numbers are not the same, check for addition or subtraction errors in your register. Then look to see that you have deducted any bank service

charges or fees from your register. Also verify that the amount of your check equals the amount you wrote in the register—this is a common place for small errors. Finally, make sure the amount recorded in your checkbook register is the same as the amount listed on the bank statement.

Organizing Paperwork

Have you heard that we're moving toward a paperless society? I certainly can't see it as I look around at our file cabinets filled with paper. A couple of years ago, in an effort to put unpaid bills in a central place yet out of sight, I bought a basket with a lid and placed it in our home office. Now the bills are stacked on top of the basket lid—it just requires too much energy to put them inside—but at least they are in one place. What can I say? We are a family of pile makers.

Deciding how to organize your bills, receipts, and bank statements is an important yet highly personal matter. Your papers should be filed in a manner that allows for easy access in case they are needed to prove a date of purchase or payment. In a file cabinet, we have a set of folders that separates bills, receipts on major purchases, medical paperwork, insurance payments, and bank statements. Papers in each category are filed chronologically in order of the date they are received or paid. If you don't have room for a permanent file cabinet, use a plastic accordion folder or a portable file box. Both can be found at discount or office supply stores.

Once a year, we clean out these files and throw out old warranties and receipts. Any statements or other documents relating to our income taxes go into a big envelope, along with the final tax returns, which are then stored away together. The Internal Revenue Service requires you to keep most of these papers for a period of three years in case you are audited. For more information on record keeping for individuals, go to the IRS website (www.irs.gov), and search for Publication 552.

Exercising Your Budget

I've heard the term *budgeting* compared to a financial "diet." Yum! Doesn't that sound appealing? I like to think of budgeting as more of a financial planning "exercise." For those who are thinking that exercising isn't much better than dieting, the good thing about this exercise plan is that you only have to work out really hard once a year—and then just do a few maintenance exercises the rest of the time.

It's important to get started as soon as possible. One mom asked, "If I want to start living on a budget, how do I save enough cash to begin? I have to have all my bills paid before I can start, right?" Wrong. Following this rationale, you would wait until you'd reached your ideal weight before starting to exercise. A budget is the tool that helps you pay off your bills and start saving for the future.

What are the top four reasons why people hate budgeting?

4. It requires some time and thought.

3. You have to sit down and plan things out.

2. It's not really fun and can seem tedious.

And the number one reason why people hate budgeting is (drum roll, please):

1. If you go to the trouble, you have to try to stick to it.

But working on a budget accomplishes several things. It shows how much you are spending in various categories. A budget helps you keep expenditures lower than the amount you earn and gives you benchmarks that can help you meet financial goals.

The first step in budgeting is *not* to arbitrarily decide how much you would like to spend each month on groceries, or gas, or clothes. Instead you need to find out where you are, financially speaking, and where you've been. You've already taken the first step by balancing your checkbook, but the real workout begins as you discover how you've been spending your money and compare that with how much you earn. Here are three workout techniques to get your finances in shape:

Aerobic (quick start). Starting now (or the end of this month), keep track of what you spend in each expense category, as well as how much you earn. The easiest way to do this is to use one side of a sheet of paper for each category and simply list your income and expenses (see next page

Diagram 5: Budget Categories*

Income

Take-Home Pay	Rental Income
Commissions/Bonuses	Alimony/Child Support
Interest/Dividend Income	

Expenses

Savings	Groceries and Dining Out
Childcare	Transportation Costs (gas, registration, maintenance/repairs, parking and tolls)
Mortgage/Rent (including property taxes)	
Insurance	
Utilities (telephone, gas and electric, water and sewer, cable or satellite TV)	Entertainment (toys and lessons, subscriptions, music and theater tickets, Internet)
Garbage	Pet Care
Yard Care	Gifts and Cards
Repairs	Charitable Contributions
Toiletries (cosmetics, medications, vitamins, shampoo, bath soap)	Personal Business (postage, office supplies, accountant)
Doctor Visits	Loan and Credit Card Payments (including interest and fees)
Clothing and Accessories	

*This is not a complete list of income and expenses. Add or subtract categories based on your family's experience.

for a list). You can use either your checkbook register or paper receipts to keep track of payments. For credit card payments, go directly to your credit card statement to separate expenses, and don't forget to create an expense category for "interest" if your bill isn't paid in full each month. After doing this for about three months, the amount you usually spend on various expenses should be apparent.

Strengthening (heavier lifting). This is basically the same as the "aerobic" exercise, except you can use financial records from the past several months to figure out your pattern of monthly income and expenses, without having to wait for more time to pass. If you didn't keep a checkbook register, the same information is available from canceled checks. A variation on this method is to target problem areas with your budgeting workout. Pick a few categories where you tend to overspend and make a detailed budget for just those expenses. (Use this approach to targeting problem areas with any of the budget workouts.)

Cross training (covering all the bases). Have you ever wondered why financial experts suggest you go through a full year's worth of financial records before preparing a budget? It's because most of us have expenses, and sometimes earnings, that occur only once a year. Some examples would be: insurance on your home or car, vacation expenses, gifts at Christmastime (or if you're one of those families with many birthdays in one month, gifts that month), wood for the fireplace, and a year-end bonus. These large, once-a-year inflows and outflows can leave you scratching your head, wondering what went wrong with that month's budget.

If you have the strength and endurance necessary to go back through a year's records, you'll come up with the most complete and accurate picture of your family's earning and spending patterns.

Creating Cash Flow Statements

Once you've "worked out" the details, it's time to take a look at the bottom line. Sir Henry Taylor said, "The art of living easily as to money is to pitch your scale of living one degree below your means."[1] Are you spending more than you earn? (Frequent bad sobs after you've reconciled your checkbook should be your first clue that this is the case.)

Simply add up all your income from the month, and subtract all your expenses. Since we are working with cash inflows (income) and outflows (expenses), this is called a *cash flow statement*. You can even use your list of budget categories (page 61) as a worksheet to write everything down. The number you get after subtracting expenses from income should be positive. If it's not, or if you'd just like to reduce your expenses and start saving for some of those goals we mentioned, it's time to thoughtfully consider where you can cut back. Let's focus on the expense side, because it's usually easier for families to reduce expenses than it is for them to significantly increase income.

Some expenses are "fixed," meaning you can't easily change the amount you spend from one month to the next (like your mortgage or car payment). The expense categories you really want to pay attention to are "discretionary," or controllable, ones, such as clothing, food, and entertainment. The money you choose to spend on these items can make a big impact on your budget.

I hesitate to give guidelines like, "Don't spend more than $10 a month on Starbucks," because the key to coming up with a workable budget is that it works *for you*. Perhaps if you don't have your coffee while running errands or on your way to playgroup, you turn into Mean Mommy. You may want to try going to Starbucks just once a week and making coffee at home the rest of the time, but you are the only one who knows how vital coffee is to your sanity and the well-being of your children.

That example illustrates the fact that we all place different levels of value on things. If you choose where to cut spending, you're more likely to be successful in sticking to your budget. Think about what you are willing to give up and what you can't live without; then look at each expense category, and set a limit for monthly spending. To increase your savings, gradually lower the budget amount for "nonessential" items, and see if you can make do with less.

Using Financial Software

Of course, good old pencil and paper work just fine in drawing up a budget, but today budgeting has also gone high-tech. Software programs like Quicken or Microsoft

Money allow you to simply enter the information from your pay stubs, checks, and bills, and your home computer will reconcile your bank statement, calculate your cash flow statement, and make comparisons to your budget in less than a second. No accounting experience is needed for one of these simple bookkeeping programs. As long as you can type and point and click, they're just as easy to use as any other piece of software.

Prices for the basic versions of these programs vary from $20 to $35 at discount stores and online, but check your home computer first. Many come with either Quicken or Microsoft Money already installed. The downside is that the programs will only work with the information put into them, so you must be disciplined about sitting down and typing in the information on a weekly or monthly basis.

Working It

At this point, most of the hard work is over! You've discovered where you are financially by following one of the recipes for balancing your checkbook, and the tough budgeting workout is over. Now what? To get financially fit, and stay that way, it's time for those maintenance exercises I mentioned earlier. Once a month, see how the amount you spent compares to your budget. Focus just on the categories where a big difference exists. What happened? Here are some possible explanations for an unexpected overage:

- You had a big one-time expense, like car repairs or a new piece of furniture.
- Your original budget amount was unreasonably low.
- You weren't as careful with your money as you can be next month.

Regardless of the reason, choose one or two of the expense categories that caused the most trouble, and work to resolve the difference. Here's an easy system to help you keep track of what you spend in each category for the first couple of months. Label the outside of a set of envelopes with your expense categories, one per envelope, and then place the amount of cash you've budgeted for that month (or pay period) into the envelopes. As you make payments, record the purchases and amounts on the outside of each envelope. When an envelope is empty, you stop spending for that category—no cheating by using a credit card. Writing everything down will help you decide how to reallocate money in your budget categories, so that your budget will meet your needs and your goals.

Staying close to your budget will make it easier to reach your financial goals, but whether that budget is etched in stone or simply a guideline is up to you. A "looser" budget plan allows you to shift money between expense categories, as long as the total amount you spend remains the same. A budget should not be a straightjacket but a tool to provide you with information to help manage your finances—flexibility is an important component of making it work. Don't allow frustration with your first few months' results to derail your commitment to get your finances under control. This is a *process* that eventually allows you to tell your money where to go, instead of just wondering where it went.

Mom's Money Makeovers

Even though budgeting may seem like a tedious, time-consuming activity, it's an essential part of getting your finances under control. The good news is that the longer you work with a budget, the easier it gets. As one mom put it, "I don't always have to write down every purchase in each expense category. Now that I'm paying attention to money matters, my budget has become so ingrained that I just mentally keep track of where we are financially."

Frugal Family Financiers and Capable Currency Managers. This chapter may have seemed like déjà vu all over again for you. Most FFFs and CCMs already have their finances under control, but you may consider making the process easier by utilizing online banking. Combine that product with computer software like Quicken, so that financial reports and comparisons can be done with the push of a finger.

Ambitious Breakeven Caretakers. If you're already balancing your checkbook (at least part of the time), it's time to make the commitment to putting together a budget. For those of you who would like some general spending guidelines, here are a few:

- 30–40 percent of your take-home pay for housing costs, including taxes, insurance, and utilities.
- 10–20 percent for food.
- 10–15 percent for car and other debt payments.
- 15–20 percent for varying expenses, like clothing, entertainment, and home repairs.
- 5–10 percent for savings.

Extravagant Home Economists. If you don't balance your checkbook and can't make heads or tails of the explanation in the "Balancing Your Checkbook" section, ask for help from someone who does this regularly. While you are learning, avoid costly fees and overdrafts on your account by padding your account with an extra money cushion. You can build this cushion by rounding up to the next dollar each check you record in your register. For example, you write a check at Wal-Mart for $30.82 but record the check amount as $31.00 in your register. Depending on the number of checks you write, this finagling can add up to a few extra bucks each month.

bank on the best 4

I still remember my first bank with great affection. It was a blue, ceramic pig decorated with flowers. I dutifully deposited my weekly allowance inside, but my favorite thing about the piggy bank was the rubber stopper underneath that I could pull out to raid, or simply count, my savings. The bank was small, but the freedom and independence it represented was mighty to that young girl.

Banking seems a lot more complicated today—and this from a banker! There are a dizzying number of financial companies and financial products available to consumers. How do you know that you are getting the most from your relationship with a financial services provider? Be a discerning consumer. You wouldn't buy the first washer and dryer you liked at the first store you visited. Take the time to shop around for the financial partner that offers the most on the products you need. Let's start with a brief description of the most common institutions competing for your business:

Banks are more full-service institutions than other financial entities are. They offer deposit accounts, loans, mortgages, investment options, business lending, and other financial services. Deposits are insured. Banks tend to offer better interest rates on loans than most other businesses do, but they are also more conservative in their lending decisions.

Credit unions were originally set up for individuals and consumers and are member owned. Though credit unions are supposed to serve a specific group of people, the lines are blurring about how a group is defined. If one family member qualifies, usually everyone can join. As with banks, deposits are insured. Fees and interest rates can be lower because credit unions are nontaxable and do not have to pay stock dividends.

Mortgage companies provide lending on real estate. They usually have more real estate financing options available than other businesses but do not offer any kind of deposit accounts.

Finance companies are mainly consumer lenders. Their interest rates are higher than at banks, but their lending practices are also less conservative. Finance companies will sometimes make loans a bank has declined.

Payday loan companies—don't go here! They offer very-short-term consumer loans, and the effective interest rate on these loans can be as high as 1,000 percent. They sometimes require collateral, but not always. You are basically borrowing against your next paycheck—what will you do the following week?

Choosing a Bank

If you're looking for a new *depository* relationship, meaning a place where you can deposit and withdraw your money, a bank or credit union is the most likely candidate. (I'll just use the term "bank" to designate both.) However, not all banks are created equal. Most prevalent are the huge bank conglomerates with names you recognize, like Wells Fargo and Chase, but there still are some small, independent banks in operation.

Both types of institutions have benefits and drawbacks. Larger banks may offer a wider variety of services, but they charge higher fees to offset the cost. If you live in a metropolitan area, a big, commercial bank with lots of ATM and branch locations may still make sense for the sake of convenience. Smaller, independent banks can provide more personalized service and attention. It's nice to have someone greet you by name—especially when that person is the gatekeeper of your money. One caution, in this age of mergers and acquisitions: independent banks are being gobbled up by bank holding companies, so you could choose an independent, neighborhood bank only to find it's under new management next month.

If you're more concerned about cost, visit several convenient bank locations, and ask for a brochure outlining their fees. Set out the brochures side by side, and do your own cost comparison. Pay the most attention to fees on the transactions and services you use regularly, like minimum account balance, ATM, and overdraft fees. While cost is a factor in the decision-making process, also consider how knowledgeable and helpful the bank staff is—especially if you are relatively new to the world of finance. Always make sure your institution is insured by the Federal Deposit Insurance Corporation. The FDIC label means that your deposits will be protected by this government entity up to a combined total of $100,000 per individual.

Checking Accounts

While checking accounts are usually structured much the same, larger banks offer several variations on those discussed below. Watch out for cute, and sometimes confusing, marketing titles that banks use for their accounts. Be a careful consumer by getting specifics on the restrictions and fees associated with any account before setting one up.

Basic checking (non-interest-bearing) account. This type of account allows you to write as many checks, have as many debit transactions, and make as many deposits as you like. It usually has a minimum balance requirement, but not always. If your balance goes below the required minimum even one time during the month, you will be charged a monthly fee. Many banks offer basic checking without fees as long as your paycheck is directly deposited into the account (done electronically by your employer).

NOW account. This type of account also allows you to have as many checks, debits, and deposits go through the account as needed, but it pays a small amount of interest each month, based on the average daily balance. There is always a minimum balance required, both to avoid fees and to earn interest, and these two balances are usually not the same.

Money market account. These accounts are technically considered to be savings accounts—they really are not set up to allow you lots of transactions. You can write a certain number of checks per month and have a few automatic debits (up to six combined), but the bank is not supposed to allow you to go beyond that. However, daily withdrawals *in person* are permitted. Because of these restrictions, you earn a higher rate of interest than with a NOW account. This is not the type of account you should use as a daily household account.

Savings Accounts

Basic savings. This is a standard savings account that allows you to have only a few transactions each month. You cannot write checks out of this account, so withdrawals must be in person or through electronic or automatic transfer. It's good for short-term savings for emergencies and big expenses like cars, appliances, vacations, repairs, insurance, and taxes. Use this type of account to accumulate funds until you have enough saved to transfer to a longer-term investment. Putting money into a basic savings account protects it by making you think before spending.

Passbook account. This is set up like the basic savings account except the bank gives you a register book for recording your transactions. The bank usually sends updated statements on this account only every six months.

Certificates of deposit. Otherwise known as CDs, these are longer-term, interest-bearing, nontransaction accounts. Typically you put a lump sum of money ($1,000 or more) into a CD for a specific time period of anywhere from three months to five years. You are not allowed to withdraw this money before the CD matures without substantial interest penalties, which means you will get all your original investment back but not all the interest you've earned. The "rules" for different types of CDs vary, so be sure to ask for thorough explanations. This is money you should put away and forget about, because you're not supposed to touch it.

Other Services

Overdraft protection. It used to take several days for your check to run through the banking system. However, with a recently instituted system named Check 21, the Federal Reserve can transfer checks into electronic debits (deductions) out of your account. This reduces the three or more days of "float" you used to have when writing a check down to a processing time of about one day. If you are not an avid checkbook balancer, Check 21 could increase the chances of overdrawing your account. Banks offer overdraft protection services to help you avoid both their fees on overdrawn accounts or returned checks and retailers' bounced check charges. There are four basic types of overdraft protection:

1. Your checking account is tied to another account at the bank, such as your savings account. When you are overdrawn, an amount sufficient to cover the deficit is transferred from the second account—usually in multiples of a predetermined amount, like $25. (So the bank would transfer $25, $50, or $75 and so on.) No additional fees are usually associated with this arrangement. However, you are allowed only three electronic transfers per month from a savings account, so your protection will have to be used sparingly.

2. The bank sets up a credit line that is tied to your account. For a small fee, monies are transferred into your account to cover any overdrafts. Even though this fee is less than what you would pay if a check actually bounced, you must remember that the credit line is a *loan* that you will have to pay back with interest.

3. A link is established between your credit card and your checking account. In the event of an overdraft, a cash advance is taken from the card and deposited into your checking account. This advance may be subject to the usual cash advance fee for your credit card, and the

whole transaction will show up on your credit card statement for payment as usual.

4. For a monthly fee of $10 to $25, your bank agrees to cover overdrafts up to a certain amount (usually less than $500). The downside to this arrangement is that the bank usually retains the right *not* to pay an overdraft at its discretion, even though you may think you're covered.

ATM cards. Today most cards are hybrids of ATM cards and debit cards that allow you to withdraw money at ATM machines.

Debit cards. Fast becoming the replacement for checks, customers use these cards at retailers like they would credit cards, but the money comes directly out of their checking account.

Automatic debits. Some businesses, like banks, insurance companies, and health clubs, offer slightly lower rates if you allow them to automatically debit your checking account for payment. A set amount is automatically deducted from your account on the same day each month or quarter, so you don't have to write a check. The downside to this arrangement is that it takes away your ability to manage the timing of your payments. In other words, you can't put the payment off for a few days when you're short on funds from paying for two unexpected doctor visits that same week!

Brokerage accounts. These are investment accounts offered by some large banks where the money is typically invested in stocks, bonds, and mutual funds and *not* covered by FDIC insurance. In these accounts, you can lose not only what you earn on your original investment, but the original investment too. Only consider this type of investing after your finances are well under control and you are looking ahead to what financial planners call "wealth accumulation."

Online Banking

When online banking was first introduced, there were many bankers who considered it a "here today, gone tomorrow" phenomenon, including yours truly. Initially, it seemed unlikely that large numbers of customers would trust their bank accounts to the Internet. I couldn't have been more wrong. Recognizing the savings to be had in paper, postage, and manpower, banks have made online banking very attractive. While the fees and balance requirements for deposit accounts are usually the same whether you bank online or not, the additional services (which are often free) add lots of value to your account. Here is a list of typical benefits to online banking:

- Checking your account balances and viewing transactions anytime.
- Transferring money between approved accounts.
- Receiving and paying bills online (no checks, stamps, or envelopes).

- Applying for a loan without having to go into the bank's offices.

- Downloading account transactions into your computer's financial management software to prepare financial and cash flow statements and make comparisons against your budget.

To overcome customer concerns about security, most firms offer reimbursements for unauthorized use of funds and for late fees on bills if payment isn't made within a certain period of time. With online bill paying, you can also set up automatic payments of equal amounts to be made on the same day each month for things like your mortgage or car payment, as well as schedule other individual bill amounts and payment dates.

It turns out that not all the banks you'll find on the Internet are insured by the FDIC. Search for your institution on the FDIC's online database by going to its website at www.fdic.gov, clicking the "Consumers" link, and selecting "Is My Bank Insured?" Finally, to make sure you can deal with infrequent but inevitable glitches, find out how easy it is to reach a real, live person at the bank for help before signing on.

Loans

An old bit of wisdom tells us, "Never a borrower or a lender be," but few of us make it through life without borrowing money for some purpose. Here are brief descriptions of the main types of personal loans offered by banks and other financial service businesses.

Installment loans. These loans can be secured by collateral (like a car) or unsecured. The length of the loan ranges from a couple of months to five years; however, most banks don't offer loans for a term of less than three months and for less than $1,000. The interest rate is usually fixed, and you make either monthly, quarterly, or yearly payments. You'll typically get a better interest rate if you can offer collateral for the loan, and banks usually offer lower interest rates and better terms than a finance company or payday lender would.

Single-payment (bullet) loans. These are similar to installment loans except that you don't make monthly payments. The entire amount is due at the maturity of the loan, usually in one year or less. You can use this type of loan when you know you will be receiving a lump sum, like a bonus, settlement, or refund, before the maturity date.

Real estate loans. There are many different kinds of real estate loans. They basically are installment loans for the purchase of a house or improvements to a house. The loan is secured by the property, which means the bank holds a mortgage against your home. If you don't pay the loan, the bank can foreclose. A down payment of anywhere from 3 to 20 percent of the purchase price of the real estate is usually required, with an average home mortgage down payment being 5 to 10 percent. Your willingness to put

up a substantial down payment makes lenders more likely
to approve your loan and may yield you a lower interest
rate.

Monthly payments are usually required at a fixed or variable rate of interest. *Fixed rate* means that the rate you are
charged on your loan will not change. On *variable-rate*
loans, the rate is tied to the bank's index and can fluctuate
by several percentage points, depending on the terms of
your loan. These fluctuations can be monthly, quarterly, or
yearly, and they affect the amount of your payments. Here's
an example: if you have a variable rate starting at 7 percent
and your loan allows a maximum rate increase of 2 percent
a year, you could conceivably be paying 9 percent the next
year and 11 percent the following year. This actually happened to many borrowers during the inflationary period
of the early 1980s. To protect your investment, make sure
you can afford payments on the loan, even at these higher
interest rates. (More on different types of mortgage loans
in chapter 8, "Get Debt Down.")

Home equity loans. Buyer beware! These loans should
really only be used for making improvements to your home
or, on a limited basis, for financial emergencies such as to
cover medical bills. They shouldn't be used to pay off credit
cards. The collateral for this loan will again be your house,
like having a second mortgage. Once the equity in your
home is gone, it's very difficult to get it back. If you have
to sell your house before paying off the loan, you will be
robbing yourself of any built-up value. The benefits of a
home equity loan are that the interest is typically deductible

on your tax return, and you can usually get a better interest rate and longer terms than with an installment loan.

Asking for a Loan

Going in to ask for a loan can be a nerve-racking experience. Comedian Bob Hope once said, "A bank is a place that will lend you money if you can prove that you don't need it." Of course, lenders wish that all borrowers could be perfectly creditworthy, but they accept the reality that this is seldom true. Lower your anxiety level and improve your chances of getting financing by being prepared to answer these questions:

1. What do you want the money for? (Be specific.)
2. How long do you want to take to pay the loan back?
3. Where do you plan on getting the money to pay it back?

Go into the meeting with some idea of the monthly payments you can afford. The rule of thumb at our bank is that fixed obligations, including the loan you are requesting, should not exceed 40 percent of gross income. Fixed obligations would include your rent or mortgage and credit card, student loan, and car payments, but not taxes, insurance, or utilities. Gross income is your income before any deductions for taxes or insurance but excluding bonuses—not your take-home pay. If you take your monthly fixed obligations, divide that number by monthly gross pay, and multiply by 100, the result should be less than 40 if you want to apply for new debt. Bear in mind that banks will loan up to this maximum, but that taxes of 15 to 25 percent added to fixed obligations of 40 percent of gross pay leaves only 35 to 45 percent for all the rest of your expenses. So it's wise for families to keep debt payments below this level. The maximum percentage varies slightly from bank to bank, but you'll save yourself some time if you do this calculation and know where you stand before making an appointment.

When meeting a lender, bring a recent pay stub and the W-2 form you used to prepare last year's taxes. (This is especially important if you are relying on irregular bonuses to pay back the loan.) After your banker talks with you about your loan request, the application process begins. For a consumer loan, you'll probably be handed a form that asks for answers to the three preceding questions and the usual personal information, like name, address, birth date, driver's license number, Social Security number, and employment status.

A lender may require you to fill out a financial statement, listing your assets and liabilities, in order to estimate your net worth. Don't be put off by this financial lingo. Assets are simply things that you own, such as bank accounts, real estate, investments, and personal property. Liabilities are things you owe others, including any loans and credit card balances. The biggest asset for most young families is the value of their home, and the largest liability is their mortgage. Net worth equals the difference of assets minus liabilities. This number is just an indication of where you are financially at one moment in time. As with net income, you want your net worth to be a positive number. However, net worth should build up over time, so don't be disappointed if your result isn't a huge number.

Answer all questions as completely and honestly as possible, and sign the application. Be up-front about any blemishes on your credit record. It's better to explain these before a lender finds them on your credit report. If you have been involved in a collection action that has been paid, dig out records for proof. Collections show up quickly on credit reports but can be slow to come off. A bank has thirty days to respond to credit applications; however, in the words of my banker husband, "If you wait that long, you've gone to the wrong place."

Before a consumer loan is made, you should receive a "truth in lending" disclosure, which tells you the total interest you'll pay over the life of the loan and the fees charged. The disclosure also shows you the *effective rate of interest*, or the interest rate taking into account fees you'll pay to get the loan. Here's a brief example: borrowing $1,000 for a short amount of time at a 13 percent interest rate with a $100 application fee might result in an actual rate of 40–50 percent to borrow the money. (In this case it would probably be more cost effective to take out a cash advance against your credit card.) It's always important to take into account both fees and interest rate, because the loan with the lowest interest rate may not be the best deal.

The loan process for mortgage loans differs somewhat. The application form you'll receive is standardized and much more detailed. There are also laws that require banks and mortgage companies to disclose more information to borrowers. For example, they must provide an estimate of what your closing costs will be (called a good faith estimate) within three days of your submitting a *completed* application with all required information.

Minimizing Fees

The most consistent complaints bank employees handle have to do with fees. Whether the charges relate to loans or deposit accounts, *everyone* hates paying them. There are three general rules for minimizing the amount of bank service charges and fees you incur:

1. **Understand the rules of your account, and don't violate them.** Ask the person opening your new account to give you "for instances" of when fees would be charged. Don't be afraid to ask questions if something seems unclear.
2. **Develop a relationship with your bank.** The longer the history and the more accounts you have, the greater the likelihood that your banker will be willing to waive or refund fees.
3. **Be a good customer.** Don't excessively overdraw your accounts or make late loan payments. A banker will look at a history of responsible behavior and be more forgiving of an occasional mistake.

If you don't qualify for a free checking account, open an account that allows you unlimited transactions for a flat monthly fee. With this fee structure, there will be no unpleasant surprises when your monthly bank statement arrives.

ATM fees can really pile up, but most banks allow customers to use ATMs the bank owns for free. Try to plan your withdrawals so that you can make it through a week with only one visit to the money machine. If you need cash, write a check for more than the amount of your purchase at the grocery or drug store.

Negotiating Skills

Many people have no idea how good or bad their credit really is, which puts them at a disadvantage when negotiating with lenders. One mom commented, "Being insecure about loans has caused me a number of problems. I accepted a car loan above the rate I should have and was placed with a company that has a reputation in the industry of providing loans to those who can't get them any other way. I discovered this when another loan officer asked why I got this particular loan where I did. I also don't know how far to negotiate and am uncertain enough to do it poorly."

Actually, moms are expert negotiators. "If you pick up your toys, then we can play a game together." "You can wear your mermaid costume to the store as long as you wear shoes with it." "If you go on a bike ride with your friend, you need to check in at home in thirty minutes."

Raising children is one long negotiation, but even with all our experience, women are less likely than men to haggle over prices, rates, and terms. Here are some general tips for successful "adult" negotiations:

- The outcome of most negotiations depends on how much research you've done beforehand.
- Begin a negotiation with good alternatives in mind.
- "No" is not the end of the discussion. Determining why the answer is no gives you a place to start working toward a compromise.
- Let the other side make the first offer, then ask for more than you think you'll get.
- Spend more time asking good questions and listening to answers rather than talking. Silence may be the best response if you don't get the answer you want. It often forces the other person to talk more and revise their position.

Most moms don't realize that almost everything is negotiable in the financial services arena. For loans, you can negotiate when they will be paid off, the interest rate, and how often you make payments. This last item is important because it allows you to fit the loan payment schedule in with your cash flow and other fixed payments, like your mortgage. On the deposit side, you may be able to negotiate a better rate on CDs if you are a good customer or have a significant amount to invest.

Remember, the larger the number of accounts, both loans and deposits, that you have at an institution, the more clout you'll have in negotiations. Before approaching your banker about a better deal, ask at least one other place for a quote, or bring in a competitor's ad and ask for the same terms or better. Bankers do value and appreciate customer loyalty, so to strengthen your rapport, give them the opportunity to match the terms of a deal. They may return the favor someday when you really need it!

Mom's Money Makeovers

It might seem that the entire banking experience is designed to intimidate the customer, from the plush carpet and marble counters to the overwhelming array of products available. These trappings often disguise the fact that banking is a service industry. Ask as many questions as needed for you to feel comfortable. Don't feel stuck with a product or an institution that isn't meeting your needs—there's usually another bank just down the street that will appreciate your business.

Frugal Family Financiers. Many people underestimate the acceptability of their credit and go to finance companies for loans because they think a bank or credit union would turn them down. If you are an FFF, you probably would qualify for a loan at a bank and save lots of money on loan interest.

Capable Currency Managers. You've already proven that you're a valued customer through your banking relationship. Don't automatically accept the first offer your banker makes for a loan. If you feel you can do better elsewhere, ask if he or she would be willing to lower your rate or give you better terms.

Ambitious Breakeven Caretakers. Even if your credit history isn't perfect, your income level should still qualify you for a decent loan rate at a bank or credit union. Your lender may agree to lower your rate if you will allow loan payments to be made by automatic withdrawal from your account. Keep working toward managing your accounts responsibly by eliminating overdrafts and limiting credit card debt and other loans, so that your banker feels more comfortable about your ability to manage your money.

Extravagant Home Economists. Getting loan after loan to consolidate your debts is not going to dig you out of a financial hole. Focus on getting your spending habits under control. We've concentrated on a lot of numbers in these last two chapters—regardless of your results, remember that *you* are not your net worth.

"lay" a nest egg   5

My husband has been skydiving. This amazes me, because I'm
the type that gets woozy looking over the side of a tall building. He has a natural affinity for risk, and heights, that I don't
share. Perhaps it's partly a function of gender—as women,
we do tend to worry more. I'm the one who mimics my own
mother by calling, "Don't run with a stick or you'll poke your
eye out!" while my husband chases the kids around brandish-
ing a stick of his own. However, whether or not you are a risk
taker is partly a matter of perspective. Growing up in a family
of cautious, conservative personalities, I was considered the
risk-taking one. I've noticed that same tendency to take risks
to a greater or lesser extent in each of my children. Have you
ever wondered what drives your "climber" to scale the bars of
the crib, the kitchen cabinets, or the backyard tree? Does he
crave the freedom, the thrill, or does he just want a cookie?

Just as each of us is willing to undertake a certain level
of risk in our personal lives, our financial selves have a risk

threshold as well, a limit beyond which we feel uncomfortable or downright woozy. Since risk is an important element of any savings plan, you should consider if the risk in any investment is worth the estimated reward. Your risk threshold may differ from that of your spouse or friends—it's part of your unique money management personality. The risk inherent in investing in the stock market—that you can actually end up with less money than you started with—may not be worth the possible reward of earning enough to be a millionaire by the time you retire. Someone who is *risk adverse* (not too keen on taking big risks) might be happier with investments that grow steadily over time, even if a smaller retirement income results.

If you've ever watched the popular game show *Who Wants to Be a Millionaire?*, you've witnessed contestants performing risk-reward analysis. There's some risk, for instance, in using a "lifeline" to consult with a friend by telephone about a response. Then, as the money prize increases and the questions get harder, each contestant must ask him- or herself: should I take the money I've earned or risk missing the next answer? You can almost see the wheels turning in the contestants' heads with each new dilemma. Similarly, every financial investment involves risk. In general, the higher the risk, the more you should expect to earn.

Starting to Save

Before we discuss the risks and rewards of various investment nest eggs, let's review where you can find the money to begin and how much you should be saving. The personal savings rate in the United States has dropped dramatically in the last fifty years. According to financial experts, we should currently be saving between 10 and 20 percent of our income for retirement and other big expenses. That's a big chunk of change for most of us. If you can't start off with such an aggressive savings plan, should you just wait until your financial situation improves? No. Remember the old adage: *a penny saved is a penny earned.* The sooner you begin putting money away, even pennies, the faster you'll start earning. Use these three principles to lay your own nest egg.

Spend less than you earn. This is the first principle of good money management—so simple that many of us overlook it. No investment plan can make up for living beyond your means. The simplest way to save money to invest is by reducing expenses. Start small by going out to eat less and shopping at sales more. Then consider bigger items, like delaying a move to a larger house or holding onto your gently used car for a couple more years.

Pay yourself first. Most people will spend what they earn. If you develop the discipline to put away $5, $25, or $50 as soon as you receive a paycheck, the money you save will yield big dividends later. The best time to begin a "pay yourself first" program is when you get a pay raise. Simply take the increase in each paycheck and put it in your savings account instead of allowing minor expenses to eat it up. To make saving even easier, set up automatic withdrawals from your paycheck or checking account. If you never see the money, you're less likely to spend it.

Make do with what's left. Though it may require restraint, saving should not be considered a punishment or a chore. Instead of thinking about what that extra money could do for you now, look forward to more financial security later.

Investment Options

Say you've saved up some money that you want to invest—it can be hard to know where to start, because the number of investment options available today is staggering. To be successful in managing your own investments, you must be willing to do two things:

1. **Educate yourself about investments.** Even though the media promotes stories of investment professionals who have lost millions, you will do a better job of investing by becoming knowledgeable. In fact, it's better to put your money into a simple interest-bearing savings account than to invest in something that you don't understand.

2. **Periodically review investments to see if they are performing as expected.** You shouldn't plan on making investments just once and leaving your money there forever. Changes in the economy, as well as in your financial situation, may dictate a different investment strategy.

Let's start the education process by looking at four of the most common types of investments.

Savings Accounts

With interest rates on basic savings accounts as low as 1.5 percent in recent years, you may question if opening a savings account is worth the trouble. Proverbs 13:11 says, "He who gathers money little by little makes it grow." While the interest you'll receive from a savings account may be less than a riskier investment would earn, it's still better than hiding your money under the mattress or burying it in a can in the backyard. We'll see later in this chapter how potentially lower-earning savings, money market, and CD accounts have a place in any investment portfolio. These savings vehicles require a small initial investment both to open and to earn interest—small enough that you can open as many accounts as you like to keep funds for different purposes separated.

Stocks

Stocks are shares of ownership in a company. The company is not obligated to pay you anything before you sell the stock; however, most companies make periodic payments, called dividends, based on the number of shares you own. The value of a stock rises and falls with the company's performance, which means that one year later your investment could be worth twenty times what you paid for it, or it could be worth nothing if the company goes bankrupt. To make an informed decision about a stock purchase, you should have a good understanding of current issues and trends in the company's industry, as well as how the company operates and what products or services it provides. Without this kind of information, or a tip from a reliable stock analyst, you will be gambling with your money.

Bonds

Bonds are basically loans made to a company, or as in the case of U.S. Treasury bonds, to a governmental entity. As with a loan, the borrower is obligated to pay you back the initial investment amount plus interest within a stated time period (known as *maturity*). There's usually a market for the purchase and sale of these investments in case you need the money before the bond matures. Bonds are rated by independent agencies according to the financial soundness of the company issuing the bonds, which translates into the company's ability to pay you back. A rating of "AAA" is the best, with a "D" meaning payments aren't being made. The higher the company's rating, the lower the interest rate you will receive on the bond because the risk of default (not paying back the bond) is lower. Three main companies rate bonds: Standard & Poor's, Moody's Investors Service, and Fitch Ratings. Your library reference desk may subscribe to the written version of their ratings, or the same information is available online (a subscription or membership fee may be required).

Mutual Funds

By investing in a mutual fund, you are purchasing shares of ownership in a pool of investments that may include only stocks, only bonds, or some combination of both. When you buy a mutual fund, you own a small part of all the stocks or bonds in the portfolio. A typical minimum investment to become part of a mutual fund is $1,000. One of the benefits of mutual funds is that, for a relatively small investment, you own a portion of a wide variety of stocks, and you don't have to go through the hassle of purchasing and managing individual shares yourself. Funds often specialize in stocks of a certain type of company or industry, for example, the stock of small companies or technology-related firms. Mutual funds are regulated by our government's Securities and Exchange Commission, but the money you invest is not insured or guaranteed.

A fund may charge several different types of fees to open and maintain an account. Some funds charge an up-front fee, called a *load*, which they deduct from the amount you send in for your original investment. Most do-it-yourself investors look for no-load funds to avoid this initial expense, but that doesn't mean they are free. Every mutual fund charges investors annual fees to cover both administrative costs and payments to the person or company managing the fund. Sometimes investors have the option to pay an account maintenance fee by check, rather than have it deducted from their account balance. A mutual fund may also charge other fees, so it's important to look at the total fund cost over a period of several years and comparison shop before you buy.

Why Diversify?

According to American artist F. McKinney Hubbard, "The safest way to double your money is to fold it over once and put it in your pocket."[1] Today there are many kinds of investment plans and models with names like Modern Portfolio Theory and Capital Asset Pricing Model, as well as a variety of investment types including stocks, bonds, real estate, savings accounts, and mutual funds. However, investments do have one thing in common: they go through cycles. This means there will be times when each type of investment does well, and there will be times when you don't want to have anything to do with an investment category.

There are three main types of assets or *asset classes* into which you can place your money: cash; fixed income assets, such as bonds; and equities, like stocks. The values of some types of assets actually go up and down inversely to one another—stocks and bonds would be an example. Many times, as the value of the stock market sharply increases, the value of bonds tends to go down. Stocks of different types of businesses can also be inversely related. You don't have to understand why this happens to see the benefits of diversifying your assets.

Compare diversification to the importance of eating a balanced diet. Say you love broccoli and know that it's good for your health. Even so, would eating just broccoli be good for you? You'd be missing out on the vitamins and nutrients in other foods, and what if the broccoli crop was destroyed by blight? You might starve. For the vast majority of investors, the key to reaching investment goals is to have a diversified investment portfolio, which in plain English means putting your money in a variety of different kinds of investments to spread the risk while earning the most you can.

Different Eggs in the Nest

The mix of assets you choose to diversify your investments should be based on the amount of time before you'll want to use the money and how much risk you are willing to take. Earlier I mentioned that investments with higher risk usually yield a higher rate of return, which is another way of saying *the more money you have the possibility of making, the greater your chances of also losing some.* Those with risk-adverse personalities who dislike gambling with their hard-earned money may wonder why they would ever chance losing some of it. The answer has to do with something you may have heard about: *inflation.*

Basically, inflation refers to the rate at which the cost of products and services increases from one year to the next. The average rate of inflation in the United States over the past five years has been a low 3 percent or less. If last year you put $10,000 into a basic savings account with an interest rate of 1 percent, the money in that savings account today (your original deposit plus interest) will not buy as much as your initial investment could have when you made it last year. That's because during the year overall prices have increased by 3 percent, while your money has only increased by 1 percent. If your investments don't earn you a greater average return than inflation, then you are actually *losing* buying power—even if your investment has increased in value.

Over the long term (ten years or more), riskier investments like stocks and bonds tend to yield much higher returns than savings accounts. Experts usually recommend that you place at least some of your money into these types of assets, if the funds won't be used until further in the future. Even if the stock market experiences a serious correction (in layman's terms, a "crash"), longer investment time horizons historically have allowed investors to recoup those losses. Deciding when you ultimately will use the money and how much you'll need determines where you should invest.

Short-Term Savings

For investment purposes, *short-term* means within the next few years, so this type of savings could be used to pay for vacations, insurance, taxes, a new car or home down payment, and other major purchases. My husband, who does a much better job of handling multiple accounts than I would, has opened separate savings accounts for many of these purposes. Keeping our funds divided helps us avoid spending them on the wrong things and makes it easier to see our progress toward each goal. Savings accounts are also good places to accumulate funds until you have enough to meet the minimum required for other types of investments (like the $1,000 needed to invest in a mutual fund). This money should be safe and accessible, which usually means in a bank savings, money market, or CD account. Even though these accounts don't earn as much, the value of riskier investments like stocks, bonds, and mutual funds can go up or down quickly, and you don't want that value to be down when you need the money.

Emergency Fund

Financial advisors recommend you maintain an emergency-fund account of three to eight times your monthly salary to help tide you over in the event of job loss, substantial medical bills, or major repairs to your home or vehicle. According to a national poll conducted by *Family Circle* magazine in 2003, only 19 percent of families with children have enough to get by for three to six months, and 74 percent are living paycheck to paycheck, so many of us have work to do in this area.[2] As with short-term savings, this money should be kept in safe, liquid accounts easily converted into cash.

College Fund

The price of college tuition has been growing much faster than the rate of inflation. During the 2004–2005 school year, the average cost of tuition, fees, room, and board for a four-year public college was $11,354, while the average total charges for a four-year private college were $27,516.[3] (For those of you still trying to catch your breath, that's between $45,416 and $110,064 for a four-year degree.) You may not be able to save enough to foot the entire bill for your child's college years, but if you put away at least one year's worth of expenses, you will have accomplished more than most families.

There are four main ways to save for your child's college education. Each has its pros and cons, including tax consequences for you and your child, and implications for receiving financial aid. Many of the rules are complicated, and to make planning ahead even more difficult, they will probably change before your child turns eighteen. Begin one of these savings programs now, but try to keep abreast of program and tax "updates" so that you can reallocate funds to best fit changing circumstances (consult an accountant if necessary).

Personal investment accounts. If you are starting ten years or more before your child enters college, it's reasonable to place at least a portion of the money you're saving into riskier investments with potentially higher returns, like mutual funds, stocks, or bonds. Tax law allows parents and grandparents to transfer a limited amount of cash and other assets to their children and grandchildren each year without tax consequences. In 2003 the limit was $11,000 per parent per child, meaning you and your spouse together could "gift" a total of $22,000 to each of your children, and grandparents could do the same.

With earnings, these gifts can add up to a significant amount of money over time, so one decision you will have to make is whether to place the money in your name or your child's. Accounts opened in your name remain under your control, but the earnings are subject to your tax rate, which is usually higher than a child's. On the other hand, once minors come of age (or reach age twenty-one if the account is opened under the Uniform Transfers to Minors Act), the money in accounts opened in their name comes under their control, whether they decide to go to college or take a trip around the world.

529 plans. States and some colleges now operate savings programs called 529 plans to help families invest funds for future college expenses. Every state now has at least one 529 plan available with different costs and investment options. Plans hire professionals to manage their funds; therefore they charge fees, which may include enrollment and annual maintenance fees. Some programs are open to residents of other states, but the program for the state where you reside may offer special tax benefits and other incentives.

Just about anyone can open a 529 account, and others besides the plan owner can make contributions. While each child must have his or her own account, a child may also have more than one. The plan owner, or donor, stays in control of the funds until they are withdrawn to pay for a child's educational expenses. Since the account is treated as an asset of the donor, funds in 529 accounts may have less impact on a child's ability to qualify for financial aid.

There are two basic types of plans: savings and prepaid. The money in 529 savings plans can usually be used for qualified expenses at any accredited college or university. However, prepaid plans are primarily designed to cover in-state tuition and may assess fees or penalties to transfer the funds to a private or out-of-state school.

The primary benefit of 529 plans is that your investment grows tax deferred, meaning you won't have to pay taxes on earnings until the money is withdrawn. Even then you may receive additional tax benefits, like paying at your child's lower tax rate. If your child decides not to attend college, you may withdraw the funds for yourself, although a penalty will be assessed on the account earnings since this would be a "nonqualified" withdrawal. For more information on 529 plans, visit your official state website or one of the following: www.savingforcollege.com or www.collegesavings.org.

Coverdell accounts. Previously known as the Education IRA, Coverdell education savings accounts are trust or custodial accounts effectively owned by your child. They allow earnings on contributions to be distributed tax free as long as they are used to pay education expenses like tuition, fees, books, supplies, and some room and board. Even though contributions are not tax deductible, there are income guidelines that determine the amount of money you can put into your child's account. The maximum contribution for a child during any tax year cannot exceed $2,000. Coverdell accounts will count as assets owned in your child's name in determining eligibility for financial aid. If you want to find out more, the IRS publishes a booklet, *Tax Benefits for Education* (Publication 970), with additional information about the rules for college investment accounts.

Educational bonds. Savings bonds to be used for college funds make excellent gifts for grandparents and other relatives who don't know what to get a child. Starting this tradition in infancy, when kids are blissfully ignorant about receiving presents, guarantees a gift your child will never break or outgrow. You can purchase savings bonds in almost every bank and credit union or online at www.treasurydirect.gov.

Savings bonds come in two basic types, Series EE and I Bonds. Bonds bought electronically come in any amount from $25 to $30,000. If you want a paper bond issued to you to hold or give as a gift, they are available from banks and credit unions in denominations of $50, $75, $100, $200, $500, $1,000, $5,000, and $10,000. The bonds are backed by the full faith and credit of the United States. They can be redeemed (turned in for cash) any time after twelve months; however, you will lose some interest if redeemed before five years. State and local entities exempt the interest earned on savings bonds from taxes, and federal income taxes are deferred until the bonds reach final maturity or you redeem them, whichever comes first.

Series EE bonds cost the purchaser only one-half of their value at maturity. In other words, a $50 bond will initially cost you $25, and a $100 savings bond will cost $50. The bonds reach their *face value*, the amount printed on the front of the bond, within seventeen years depending on interest rates, but the bonds can continue earning interest for thirty years from the date of purchase. Depending on income level, you may be able to exclude all or part of the interest earned on EE bonds from your income for tax purposes when you cash the bonds in, if the bonds are in your name and the money is used to pay for college tuition and fees.

I Bonds are available in the same denominations as Series EE Bonds, but you purchase them at face value, meaning you'll pay $50 for a $50 bond. The bonds accrue interest at a rate that is adjusted twice a year to keep up with inflation, so the value of your investment won't decline over time.

Retirement Fund

Are you counting on Social Security to pay for your golden years of retirement? Analysts project that the Social Security system will be bankrupt *before* it's time for you to get your share. And according to the Medicare trust fund trustees, without reform the Medicare trust fund will become insolvent in the year 2019.[4] Bummer! Experts estimate most of us will need to continue receiving between 70 and 80 percent of the salary we earn at the time we retire to maintain a comfortable standard of living in our golden years. Saving for retirement has become a necessity, not a luxury.

A mom once asked my opinion on the single best thing she could do to prepare for retirement, and my response was, "Start saving money as soon as you can." In fact, while putting aside funds for your child's college education is important, it's more crucial to prepare for your own future. Your child will likely have access to other resources like scholarships, student loans, and part-time jobs, while, if the previous statistics hold true, you may not. Even if kids have to rely on other sources of income during their college years, most would probably find that preferable to supporting you later when they have kids of their own to worry about.

Many financial websites offer free retirement calculators to help determine how much you should be saving to meet your financial retirement goals. Do a search for the keywords "retirement calculators" or go to CNN's or USA

Today's money pages (cgi.money.cnn.com or www.usatoday
.com/money/front.htm), click on "calculators," and follow
the step-by-step instructions. When asked to plug in estimated returns on your investments, use these average rates
from the period from 1926 to 1997: 11 percent per year
for stocks, 5.3 percent per year for bonds, and 3.8 percent
per year for cash in deposit accounts.[5]

Your employer's 401(k) program is the first place to
start saving for retirement. These plans offer tax benefits, and employers often match at least a portion of the
funds you save. Many programs allow you to choose
where your money will be placed from a list of possible
investments.

Those not employed outside the home can still take advantage of tax deductions available by opening an IRA at
a bank or with a mutual fund. Depending on your income,
even if you've already made the maximum tax-deductible
contribution to a 401(k) plan, you can still save additional
money (not tax deductible) in an IRA.

According to our own financial planner, if you have
managed to save some money on your own and would like
to begin laying a retirement nest egg, probably the best
place to start is with a mutual fund. Hundreds of mutual
fund organizations exist, but if you put your money in a
broad-based diversified fund with a good long-term record
run by one of about twenty really large, very old, highly
competent firms, your investment will probably do well.
Examples of such firms include American Funds, T. Rowe
Price, Fidelity, and Scudder. If you want to investigate the

returns of various funds on your own, several financial magazines publish annual comparisons of mutual fund performance. Visit your local library and look through the June or July issues of *Fortune* magazine for the most recent year, the February issue of *Money*, or the August issue of *Kiplinger's Personal Finance*. If you prefer to go online, visit www.morningstar.com for similar information.

Although mutual funds automatically represent a somewhat diversified investment, the savvy investor will eventually hold a couple of different types of mutual funds to increase his or her returns. You may want to complement a stock fund with a bond fund, for instance. Some companies simplify this process by offering "fund families" made up of a variety of different kinds of funds. Investing with the fund family allows you to transfer money between funds with fewer paperwork hassles, and you'll receive just one consolidated statement on all your accounts.

Remember that when investing, patience is a virtue. Over the short term, the financial markets will determine your results, but over the longer term, the skills of the professionals managing the mutual fund will begin to show. Don't jump ship if your first year's returns are disappointing. Three years is a minimum period of time to see what a fund manager can do for you.

Financial Planners Revisited

As a small investor, you can adequately manage your portfolio, but you may prefer to turn the job over to a professional. Remember that financial planners make their living through the fees they charge, and that can leave clients feeling nickeled-and-dimed to death. This mom lamented, "My experience so far has been that they are more interested in charging fees than giving financial direction and advice." When paying commission fees, you are paying for advice, so if your financial planner isn't providing the level of service or quality of information you expect, it's time to look elsewhere.

Before hiring a financial planner, be sure to ask these questions:

- What are your credentials, and how did you earn them?
- What kinds of products can you sell me and from which companies?
- Can you give me the names and numbers of several investors like me to call as references?
- How are you paid?

Give All You Can

This may seem like a strange place to discuss giving money away. We're talking about saving and investing, right? But tithing and giving money to worthy causes is simply another kind of investment. By giving, we invest toward a goal we embrace, whether that's a healthy church community or a cure for breast cancer. It's not a mistake that John

Wesley included giving as one of his three rules of money management. Try recalling your feelings the last time you gave to someone truly in need. Did you feel a sense of accomplishment, of gratitude that you were able to help? We know it's more blessed to give than to receive, because we feel that glow in our hearts.

The Bible calls on us to honor God with 10 percent of our "firstfruits," the first of our earnings. This percentage is not intended as a stick with which to beat yourself. Second Corinthians advises, "Each man should give what he has decided in his heart to give, not reluctantly or under compulsion, for God loves a cheerful giver" (9:7). However, when funds are tight, most of us restrict our giving to the First National Bank of Me. We become our own favorite charity! Compare our reliance on money with the security God provides, which is available to each of us regardless of how much or how little we have. Our pastor shared this quote from another church leader who was preparing to pass around the collection plate: "O God, no matter what we say or do, this is what we *really* think of you." By tithing, we truly have the opportunity to put our money where our mouth is.

Other requests for donations fill our mailboxes and tie up our telephone lines. How do you know which ones are legitimate and which of those channel the greatest proportion of your donation to helping others? The Federal Trade Commission suggests following this list of precautions to ensure that your donations reach the people you want to help:

- Ask for written information. A legitimate charity will tell you how your donation will be used and provide proof that it is tax deductible.

- Call the charity to find out if it's aware of the solicitation and has authorized the use of its name.

- If the telemarketer claims that the charity will support local organizations, call the local groups to verify.

- Don't provide any credit card or bank account information until you have reviewed all information from the charity and decided to donate.

- Ask for a receipt showing the amount of the contribution and stating that it is tax deductible.

- Avoid cash gifts, which can be lost or stolen. Instead, pay with a check made out to the beneficiary, not the person soliciting.[6]

Other places to check up on a charity include your state attorney general's office or a local consumer protection agency, like the Better Business Bureau. These national organizations also monitor charities:

BBB Wise Giving Alliance
(703) 276-0100
www.give.org

American Institute of Philanthropy
(773) 529-2300
www.charitywatch.org

Dealing with finances involves so much of our head and pocketbook, but giving allows us to consider money matters with our heart. The size of your gift matters much less than the fact that you are sharing your resources with those less fortunate. Poet Walt Whitman wrote, "The habit of giving only enhances the desire to give." Try investing in others—one good gift often begets another.

Mom's Money Makeovers

It's ironic that the time when you most need to save is also the time when you typically have the least amount of money available. The hardest part of any savings plan is often getting started, but beginning with even a small amount encourages you to continue saving and to increase your investments as your resources permit. By investing, you take care of your money so that later it will take care of you.

Frugal Family Financiers. If you have been squirreling away your savings haphazardly, it may be time to review your investment strategy, on your own or with a professional, to improve your results. Remember that, while saving is very important, there's little point in denying yourself to the point of being miserable. None of us knows what the future may hold, so use some of your hard-earned money to live richly today.

Capable Currency Managers. You or your spouse may already be contributing to a 401(k) plan at work. Consider how much you are investing, and think of ways to increase that amount. The next time you receive a raise, why not funnel that increase into some type of long-term investment instead of spending it? Choose a different type of investment than you already have in order to diversify.

Ambitious Breakeven Caretakers. Some people have extra money taken out of their paycheck, over and above what's needed to pay taxes, in order to receive a refund after filing their tax return. Since you earn nothing on the extra money held during the year by Uncle Sam, this is not the best way to save. However, if the refund is to be used for short-term savings, you'll only lose a little interest as long as you're disciplined enough to put that money away when it arrives. The next time you receive a large payment like a tax refund or bonus, be sure to invest at least some of that money to jump-start your nest egg.

Extravagant Home Economists. Start putting a small amount of money away in an investment where the money is difficult to withdraw, like an IRA at a local bank or in small-denomination savings bonds. By watching this money grow, you may be inspired to save more, and you'll definitely feel better about your future.

basics of credit 6

"Just use your credit card," my daughter piped up on a recent shopping trip. I had opened my wallet to discover it empty of both cash and checks.

When I explained that we try to avoid using plastic, she asked, "Why?" Patiently, I told her that we wanted to make sure we could pay off what we charged.

My daughter's response was a confused, "You have to pay for it?" I'm not sure what surprised me more, her lack of understanding that you can't get something for nothing, or that it actually occurred to my daughter to pay with a credit card. Her innocent comment brought home the fact that the use of credit permeates all our lives.

If our mail is any indication, my husband and I have excellent credit. In one week alone, we received a combined total of four credit card applications. Unfortunately, the basics of credit are not that simple. Credit card companies don't shower you with these love notes because of your sterling reputation; they solicit your business because they want to make money. Credit providers of all types earn their living by taking advantage of a disease that afflicts many of us today: See it, Want it, Buy it syndrome (or SWB for short). Read through the following list of some symptoms of SWB, and see if any apply to you:

- You use shopping as therapy.
- One or more of your credit cards are "maxed out."
- Your conversations gravitate toward things you'd like to buy.
- You receive five or more catalogs in the mail each week.
- Your house feels cluttered with too much stuff.

Oh my, I'm three for five. How about you? From reading the introduction to this book, you know that I have had problems with credit, and since misery loves company, I am not alone. A study by the American Bankers Association in 2003 showed that, for the first time in history, payments with plastic exceeded payments with cash and checks. According to the *Wall Street Journal*, "When people pay with plastic, they tend to spend more—often more than they have in the bank. Thus, credit cards also have fueled an explosion in consumer debt."[1] Evidently children are not the only ones who have trouble understanding credit! Between bank credit cards and store credit cards, the average family holds about thirteen pieces of plastic, and those who carry over a balance on their cards each month have an average of $9,000 in credit card debt.[2]

Too Much Credit?

See it, Want it, Buy it syndrome leads to an overreliance on plastic. Some warning signs that your credit is not being managed responsibly are

- Making only the minimum payment month after month
- Making important payments late (such as rent or mortgage)
- Using money from one lender to pay another
- Applying for or accepting new credit cards because credit limits on your current cards have been exhausted
- Running out of cash often
- Working overtime or a second job to cover food, housing costs, and other living expenses

Credit card companies don't make self-control easy. If you're preapproved for a card, that must mean they've checked you out and feel you deserve more credit, right? Wrong! Even if an application is stamped "preapproved," the final approval and terms for a credit card are not set until the company receives and verifies the additional information you send. Even then, many credit providers err on the liberal side. Someone we know managed to run up $65,000 of credit card debt on eight to ten cards, without ever having a late payment, by constantly transferring balances to cards with introductory offers of 0 percent interest and continuing to make minimum payments. Unfortunately, this house of cards eventually came crashing down and resulted in him having to take out a loan, secured by his *father's* home, to pay off the credit card debt. Excessive debt also prevented this big spender from buying a house of his own for at least five years.

Before you sign on the dotted line for any type of credit, it may help to remember that purchasing things in this manner is a privilege, not a right. Take a look at this sobering example of the true cost of credit card debt. If you have a balance of $4,000 on a credit card with an interest rate of 18 percent and make minimum payments of $100 a month, it will take you over five years to pay off that balance, and in that time you will have paid about $2,200 in interest. Talk about stealing your financial future! If you want to figure out how long it will take to repay credit card debt at various interest rates and monthly payment amounts, do an Internet search for the keywords "credit card calculator," or visit www.bankrate.com.

Responsible Credit Management

Now that we've established how credit can get you into trouble, my next statement may shock you. *All this negativity doesn't mean that credit doesn't have its place.* Managing credit correctly is an important life skill. If you're tempted to cut up and throw away your credit cards, put the scissors down for a minute. Certainly those with credit card debt should cease and desist using their cards immediately. If the only way you can stop charging is to get rid of them, then cut away. However, if your credit is relatively good, judicious use of a credit card can give your lifestyle a boost—but not in the way you may think.

I've already mentioned that insurance companies look at credit reports before quoting you a rate. Did you know that many potential employers also check credit reports when hiring, and apartment companies use these reports to qualify renters? Having no credit history can be just as detrimental as a bad credit history. Here's another reason for learning to manage your credit cards: plastic truly is the wave of the future. Companies are testing the viability of transferring paychecks directly onto a credit card. Those of you with credit control issues may shudder at the possibility of *having* to use a credit card for everything. But even if you manage to live your life without plastic, your children will almost certainly need credit management skills, best taught by your modeling and instruction.

While credit cards get more media attention, it's just as important to act responsibly with respect to other credit accounts. In my *Oxford Essential Dictionary*, credit is defined as the "power to obtain goods [and services] before payment." Any time you use something before paying for it, you have been extended credit—this includes utility services, contracts with cell phone companies and Internet service providers, and medical services. Potential creditors do look at your history of payments on these types of accounts (in addition to credit card, checking, and loan accounts) in deciding whether or not to offer credit and on what terms.

Credit Reporting

Not sure about the current state of your credit? Find out where you stand by ordering a copy of your credit report. There are three major credit bureaus:

Equifax
www.equifax.com
1-800-685-1111

Experian
www.experian.com
1-888-397-3742

TransUnion
www.transunion.com
1-800-888-4213

Under the Fair and Accurate Credit Transactions Act (FACT Act), you are entitled to one free credit report from each credit bureau in a twelve-month period. To request this free annual disclosure, visit www.annualcreditreport .com or call toll-free 1-877-FACT-ACT.

Additional single reports from one credit bureau will cost between $9 and $15, or you can order a "3-in-1" report for $30. If you are turned down for credit because of your credit report, you will receive an "adverse action" notice from the creditor. You are then entitled to a free copy of your credit report from the credit bureau that provided a less-than-glowing credit history.

There may be errors on any credit report, and you can, and should, dispute these or ask to have them corrected. Under the Fair Credit Reporting Act, both the credit bureau and the company that provided the information are responsible for correcting inaccuracies on your report, which means

- Information you dispute that cannot be verified must be deleted from your file
- The credit bureau must correct wrong information in the report
- Incomplete information must be completed by the credit bureau
- Accounts belonging to someone else must be deleted from your report

Certain procedures should be followed when disputing credit report information in order to safeguard your legal rights. As a first step, call the credit bureau; then follow up with a letter including copies of any supporting documentation. The Federal Trade Commission provides more information in a document titled "How to Dispute Credit Report Errors," available on its website at www.ftc.gov/bcp/conline/pubs/credit/crdtdis.htm, or look on each credit reporting agency's website for information on submitting a dispute.

What Creditors Want to See

If you plan on ever borrowing money, you must pay attention to your credit status. What do potential creditors want to see on your credit report? First, they do not want to see collection actions, foreclosures, repossessions, or a slow payment history. Creditors do want to see that you pay your credit obligations on time. They want to see that the balances you carry on credit cards are not excessive. (Remember from chapter 4, "Bank on the Best," how larger balances translate into higher payments, and you want to keep your monthly fixed obligations at 40 percent of your monthly gross pay or less?)

The next point creditors consider is how much credit you have available. Your credit report lists most open credit accounts—including all those department-store cards you opened to get the initial 10-percent discount and never used again. If you haven't actually called the credit card company and asked them to close your account, the card will likely show up with an available line of credit. Companies may consider that available credit as potential debt in deciding whether or not to extend you additional credit. This is particularly true if you are a borderline borrower.

Credit reports also provide more information of interest to potential creditors: the names of other businesses that have checked your credit. These inquiries remain on your report for two years. When potential creditors see that several credit providers have accessed your credit report, this can raise a red flag about your current financial status. Having several inquiries on a credit report can mean a consumer is out shopping for credit and may already have new debt that has yet to show up on the report.

Your credit report shows your credit limit with each creditor (usually mortgage, auto loans, and revolving credit cards), your current balance, your current monthly payment amount, and the highest balance you've had on that account. If your report shows you've paid on time, you've never reached your credit limit, and your current balance is low, that's an indication that you know how to manage your credit. While credit reports show payment history on credit cards for the past twenty-four months or more, other credit blemishes like collection actions and bankruptcies remain on the report for at least seven years.

One tricky aspect of a credit report is that not all creditors report their experiences, or they only report when there's a problem. Companies falling in this category generally include doctors' offices, hospitals, and utility companies. These businesses turn late payers in to collection agencies, who then report that the account is in collection. For example, even if you've paid your phone bill on time for ten years and then can't pay, only the collection will show up on your credit report—not all the other on-time payments. Obviously it's important to make arrangements with these types of companies *before* your account gets turned over to a collection agency in order to avoid the collection showing up on your credit report.

Credit Scoring

If you've never wanted to be reduced to just a number, you may find the concept of credit scoring disconcerting. A credit score is a single number based on factors such as bill-paying history, the number and type of accounts you have, late payments, collection actions, outstanding debt, and the age of your accounts. This number theoretically assesses the likelihood a borrower will repay a debt. Credit scoring has become the new standard for use by businesses such as banks, mortgage lenders, and insurance companies. The higher your credit score, the better the terms, rate, and amount of credit you will be entitled to—scores over seven hundred will earn you the best terms from creditors. You can find out your credit score, for a fee, from the same credit reporting agencies that will send you a copy of your credit report.

Credit Repair

If your credit doesn't make the A list, don't despair. With time and discipline, it is possible to repair your credit, because creditors pay more attention to recent payment history than to past mistakes. Nothing makes as big a difference in your credit standing as paying bills on time and paying more than the minimum, if possible. This is the first, and biggest, step to take toward improving your credit.

The next step toward financial health is to keep a checking account in good standing at a local bank, which means no overdrafts. Eventually, you can parlay this responsible behavior into some type of credit. For example, a banker may give you a small loan, even when you can't get credit any other way, based on a positive, consistent depository relationship. (If you do pursue a small loan as a way to improve your credit, make sure your lender sends payment histories to a credit reporting agency—not all banks do.)

Those with damaged credit often feel trapped in a Catch-22—they can't get credit because of a poor credit history, but their credit report won't improve unless they have credit and manage it responsibly. However, even those who have made serious financial mistakes in the past can begin to reestablish credit with one of these suggestions.

Cosigned loan. If your credit doesn't merit loan approval, a lender may still consider the request if someone with good credit is willing to sign for the loan with you. This "cosigner" will be equally responsible for repayment of the debt, so carefully consider your ability to make the required payments before putting someone else's finances on the line.

Secured credit card. Several companies will provide you with a credit card if you open a deposit account with them equal to the amount of your credit limit. There's no risk for the company, because the card is covered with the cash in your account. You can improve your credit with such a card by charging small amounts each month—only as much as you can pay off each time.

Department-store and gasoline credit cards. It's often easier to get approved for one of these types of cards. Finance rates may be higher than on a bank card, however, so be sure not to carry a balance over from one month to the next.

Do not be taken in by companies claiming they can "fix" your credit report for a fee. There is no fast and easy way to repair your credit history. Just as with any damaged relationship, it takes time and effort to rebuild creditors' trust. As you work to reestablish your credit, request a copy of your credit report each year to see how it's improving and that collections you have resolved show up as paid. Mending your credit won't happen overnight, but many creditors are willing to give you a second chance, and sometimes a third.

Mom's Money Makeovers

Consumers often view credit as an enemy to be vanquished. In truth, credit is simply a financial tool that can be either good or bad depending on the manner in which it is used.

Frugal Family Financiers. Keep at least one credit card open. Revolving credit card accounts can carry more weight on your credit report, and credit score, than installment payments on a car or home. Even one card increases creditors' confidence in your ability to manage debt beyond just fixed payments.

Capable Currency Managers. Those with good credit ratings are usually inundated with credit card offers. However, you will not improve your credit score by jumping from one card to the next. Research which card offers you the best terms, and plan on holding onto it for several years.

Ambitious Breakeven Caretakers. If you have a blemished credit past, don't panic. Creditors do take into account factors other than the information on a credit report. The credit application you fill out provides information about job stability and income level, as well as listing assets that could be sold and used to repay the debt if needed.

Extravagant Home Economists. If you've decided to improve your credit status by cutting up cards you rarely use, be sure to call the companies that issued the cards and ask that they be canceled as well. Potential creditors like to see the words "Account closed at consumer's request" on a credit report. If you simply cut up the card, the account stays open until the vendor chooses to inactivate it, which could be several years after the last transaction, or never!

who stole my identity?   7

Imagine receiving a telephone call from a creditor asking about a large number of charges on a credit card in your name. Pretty scary stuff—especially when you never applied for, or received, such a credit card! My sister, who has excellent credit, was the first person I knew to become a victim of one of the fastest-growing crime waves: identity theft. Here's her story:

> A representative of a major department store called and said they really needed to talk to me about some charges on my store-brand VISA card. The number for the credit card I had did not match the number of the card they were questioning, which they said had been opened a couple of months ago. I told them that I had not opened a new card in a long time, nor had I authorized anyone else to use any of my credit cards. The person on the phone then informed me that someone had charged $4,500 worth of merchandise to this card that was in my name. When I

asked what I should do, they gave me a list of companies and organizations to contact, beginning with credit agencies, the police, the IRS, and the Postmaster General. I ended up having to take a day off from work to contact everyone, including all my other credit card companies and businesses handling my financial accounts. It's hard to get over the feeling that you've been violated.

This story had a happy ending because my sister was notified of the problem before any other incidents of theft occurred. Still, the experience was a sobering one for our family. My sister hadn't engaged in any of the behaviors that identity theft experts warn against. It turns out that a preapproved credit card application was sent to an address she had moved from two years prior. Someone at that address filled out the application, forged her signature, and requested that his or her name be added as an approved signer on the account. Voilà, instant credit!

We expect children to play at being someone else, but that fantasy is something you are supposed to outgrow. Not so, according to the Federal Trade Commission (FTC), whose September 2003 "Identity Theft Survey Report" estimates that over 9 million people were victims of some sort of identity theft during the prior year.[1] The FTC defines identity theft as the stealing of personal information such as your name, Social Security number, credit card number, or other identifying information, without your permission, to commit fraud or other crimes.[2] People rarely realize they've been victimized until a credit request is denied or they receive a phone call from a creditor. By the time you discover the theft, the problems it causes can take months or years to straighten out.

Getting the Goods

Ever pondered what the world would be like if lawbreakers used their brains and energy for good instead of evil? Rarely is the ingenuity of the criminal mind more apparent than in identity theft. One of our bank's customers reported this scam:

> Someone called and said they were with a governmental agency investigating identity fraud in my name. The caller said he needed my checking account and Social Security numbers to verify whether or not the fraud had occurred, so I gave them to him. Apparently the caller then used the information to take several hundred dollars out of my account. Now, I'm not disciplined about reconciling my checkbook each month, so I didn't discover the money was missing. The next month, after I'd received my paycheck, several hundred more dollars disappeared from my account. This went on a total of five times before I found out what was happening.

Identity thieves use methods like these to gain access to your personal information (and the list keeps growing):

- Stealing your purse or wallet with a checkbook and credit cards inside.

- Taking the mail out of your mailbox, either before outgoing mail is picked up by your mail carrier or after your mail has been delivered.
- Going through your garbage to look for bank and credit card statements, preapproved credit card offers, bills, or medical invoices you haven't shredded.
- Posing as a landlord, employer, or someone else with a legal right to your credit report.
- Completing a change-of-address form to divert your mail to another location.
- Posing as a business that informs you, via telephone or email, that your account information has been compromised or lost and needs to be reentered.

Once your identity has been stolen, thieves can trade on the name and credit you have worked so hard to maintain. All those things you always wanted to buy but didn't, because you weren't sure how to pay for them—identity thieves have no such moral constraints. Why should they? You will handle the calls from creditors and embarrassments at the checkout counter in the thieves' place. With pilfered information, they may wreak havoc with your personal life and your finances.

Banking. Whether they steal one personal check and alter the amount to make the check larger or get hold of a box of new checks, thieves have access to your address, the bank's account and routing numbers, and perhaps your signature as well. They then can drain your accounts with checks or a debit card and continue writing more bad checks (sometimes with counterfeit checks). With your banking information, thieves can apply for new car loans or for lines of credit from other lenders. A computer-savvy fifteen-year-old in our area obtained an adult's Social Security and bank account numbers and used the information to set up an Internet porn site. The money to set up the site was debited directly from the adult's checking account. Much to his surprise, he discovered the theft upon opening his next bank statement.

Credit cards. Who hasn't dreamed of an extravagant spending spree with someone else's money? Identity thieves live the dream, often starting with purchases like big-screen TVs or computers that they can easily resell. They may use your stolen credit cards or open new credit card accounts in your name. Either way, it usually takes time before you discover you have a problem.

Services. With personal information, a thief can establish traditional phone service or get a cell phone. Leases for apartments, offices, and cars have been approved with false documentation. The most common type of identity theft in our area results from scam artists placing new utility service in the name of a former spouse, boyfriend or girlfriend, or relative. The person whose name is on the account usually doesn't find out about the charges and delinquent fees until he or she applies for some type of credit or receives a notice of a lawsuit for nonpayment.

Legal issues. Filing bankruptcy in your name allows identity thieves to avoid eviction or paying bills. Thieves have even used the names and Social Security numbers of their victims upon arrest. Arrest warrants are then issued in the victims' names when the thieves jump bail. Drivers whose licenses have been suspended, yet who still operate a vehicle, may say they don't have their license in the car when pulled over for a traffic stop. Instead they give the name and memorized license number of a relative or friend, who then receives the traffic summons in the mail and must prove his or her innocence.

The consequences of this violation of your privacy range from seriously inconvenient to financially catastrophic. Many victims find themselves unable to get credit of any kind: mortgage loans, utility accounts, credit cards, medical insurance, auto insurance, student loans, and tuition assistance. Their current and future employment could be at risk—and that's not even taking into account the hours spent resolving problems (an average of between fifteen and sixty hours, according to the FTC).[3]

Your First Clue

If you want to contain the damage done by identity thieves, it's crucial to limit the amount of money you could lose. Time is of the essence in reporting identity theft and thereby restricting your legal and financial exposure after personal information has been stolen. Many times, unsuspecting individuals have no idea of the theft until money has been lost, but certain clues indicate that your personal information is compromised.

Like my sister, you could receive a call from a company or debt collector about merchandise or services you didn't purchase. Being turned down for a loan or a new credit card when you feel your credit history warrants approval could be another clue. Most of us consider it a good day when we pick up the mail and find no bills included, but not receiving a bill or other mail you're expecting might mean it has been rerouted to a thief's address. Don't be afraid to call a company and ask about the postmark date of correspondence or subscriptions.

What to Do When It Happens

If you feel you have been a victim of identity theft, taking immediate steps to inform the companies with whom you do business can limit your liability. For example, if you report lost or stolen checks to your bank, they can block payment on the check numbers involved, or your account can be closed to prevent tampering with your funds. Those who suspect credit card fraud should call all three credit reporting agencies and ask that a "Fraud Alert" be placed on their file so no new credit can be granted without their personal approval.

Here are the numbers for the agencies' fraud hotlines:

TransUnion	(800) 680-7289
Equifax	(800) 525-6285
Experian	(888) 397-3742

The credit bureaus should also send you copies of your credit reports free of charge, which you need to review carefully for any incorrect changes of address, accounts you didn't open, and unauthorized charges. Notify credit bureaus by telephone and in writing of any inaccuracies, and call the companies that are reporting information you feel is in error. When speaking with customer service representatives, ask them to supply you with forms to dispute any transactions. As an alternative, the FTC has an Identity Theft Affidavit available at www.ftc.gov/bcp/conline/pubs/credit/affidavit .pdf that businesses may accept; however, some might require you to use their own fraud-dispute forms. File an identity theft report with your local police department, and keep a copy. Creditors may request copies from you to validate your claims. Send any correspondence by certified mail, return receipt requested. To ensure there's no new fraudulent activity, check your credit reports several times during the first year after the theft.

Immediately call the issuers of all credit cards that are missing or have unauthorized charges, including ATM cards, and close the accounts. Time is of the essence here. Liability in cases of credit card fraud is limited to $50 if you contact the creditor by mail within sixty days from when the first bill containing the fraudulent charge was mailed to you. The $50 limit on liability for ATM cards is only in effect for two days after discovering the card lost or stolen, so report such an incident immediately by phone or in person.

If you open new accounts, use different Personal Identification Numbers (PINs) and passwords. Many companies ask for your mother's maiden name as a means of verification—switch to another password instead (*not* part of your birth date, phone number, or Social Security number).

Bank accounts and credit cards are obvious targets for thieves, but other companies and agencies should also be apprised of this type of fraud:

- Social Security Administration (fraud hotline: 1-800-269-0271).
- U.S. Postal Inspection Service (call your local post office for the district office nearest you).
- Department of Motor Vehicles.
- Investment companies with whom you have accounts.
- Toll-road pass distributors.
- Your employer's human resources department.

The Federal Trade Commission is the federal clearinghouse for identity theft victim complaints. You can file your own complaint on the Internet by visiting www.consumer.gov/idtheft or by calling 1-877-ID-THEFT (438-4338). FTC counselors can also provide information to help settle disputes resulting from the theft. By maintaining a *secure* database of the particulars of identity theft cases, the FTC assists other law enforcement agencies and departments in their investigations.

The more thorough the documentation you keep on your case, the better your chances of resolving problems caused by identity theft. Keep a file with copies of all correspondence you send or receive and any forms you've filled out. When speaking with anyone by phone, write down the person's name, what he or she said, and the date of the conversation. If someone requests documents from you, be sure to send copies, never originals.

Practice Prevention

Given the number of times a day you share personal information, it may be impossible to completely safeguard yourself from identity theft. However, by taking the following fifteen protective steps, you can lessen the chances of it happening to you:

1. Store new, unused checks and canceled checks, if your bank still includes them in your statement, in a safe place.
2. Keep complete documentation of all credit cards, loans, investments, and previous addresses and employers in a safe place like a safety deposit box (preferably out of the house).
3. Keep your Social Security card in a similarly secure location, and only give out your Social Security number when absolutely necessary.
4. Don't give out personal information on the phone, by mail, or through the Internet unless you're the one who

initiated the contact. Verify company representatives by calling the customer service number on your card or account statement or in the phone directory. Don't rely on a number provided by the contact, which may be set up to lend credibility to a scam.

5. Invest in a small, home paper shredder to run all personal documents, receipts, and applications through before discarding. Think of it as an investment in our environment too, because shredded paper makes great packing material for mailing packages.

6. If your mail is delivered to an unlocked box, try to pick it up as soon as possible after delivery. Take items you want mailed to the post office, or put them in an official post office collection box whether or not you have your own mailbox. Be sure to place a hold on mail service at your local post office when going on vacation.

7. Don't carry around more checks or credit cards than you really need. Never keep your Social Security card, PIN numbers, or passwords in your wallet.

8. Once a year, check your credit record with the three major credit bureaus (see the contact information in chapter 6, "Basics of Credit").

9. Contact your bank or credit card company if you receive a suspicious telephone or email inquiry asking for account information to "verify a statement" or "award a prize."

10. Take the time to carefully review all bills and statements you receive. Promptly report any errors or questionable charges.

11. When organizations and companies ask if they may share your personal information with others, just say no. Many websites offer an "opt-out" choice to limit the distribution of your information to others for promotional purposes.

12. Register with the National Do Not Call Registry to reduce telemarketing calls at home by calling 1-888-382-1222 or visiting www.donotcall.gov. Reduce the amount of "junk" mail you receive by registering with the Direct Marketing Association's Mail Preference Service at www.the-dma.org (click on "For Consumers") or sending a letter to: Mail Preference Service, Direct Marketing Association, P.O. Box 643, Carmel, NY 10512.

13. Update computer virus-protection software regularly—most virus-protection programs do this automatically when you log on with your Internet service provider. Computer operating system companies, like Microsoft, are also constantly developing security updates and patches you can download from their websites to make your computer more secure from outside trespassers.

14. When placing orders or submitting information over the Internet, look for the "lock" icon on the status bar, and make sure the lock is closed. This symbol indicates that your information is secure during transmission. If your computer tells you that a site is not secure, get the company's phone number and call instead.

15. Before you sell or donate your computer, delete any personal information stored on it, and be sure the files are unrecoverable.

Adults are not the only ones susceptible to identity theft; thieves target children as well. Help your kids avoid blemishes on their credit before they have a chance to get a card of their own! Keep their birth certificates, Social Security cards, and other important documents in a safe location with your own.

Mom's Money Makeovers

Information about identity theft applies to all money management personalities, but the probability of the type of theft differs according to how you handle money matters.

Frugal Family Financiers and Capable Currency Managers. As we've seen, even those without a wallet full of credit cards can become identity theft victims. Have you ever seen your credit report? This might be a good time to request a copy and check for any inaccuracies or unusual activity, especially if you have moved recently.

Ambitious Breakeven Caretakers and Extravagant Home Economists. Be sure you have all pertinent information on credit cards, loans, bank accounts, and investments stored in a secure place. Call companies whose credit cards you seldom use, and ask that they be canceled to reduce your risk in case of theft.

get debt down 8

"I just don't know how everybody can afford huge homes, new cars, and keeping up with their neighbors in this day and age. Does everyone just have major debt and struggle to pay their bills, or are people making a lot of money, spending it all, and hoping they don't get laid off?" a young mom asks.

I can relate. I frequently ask our local bank president, who is also my husband, the same questions, and all too often he answers, "Yes, and yes."

Living with significant debt is like having a two-thousand-pound gorilla on your back—it's big, dark, and unpredictable. The weight bears down on you and eventually affects every aspect of your life. You start acting in ways that would never have occurred to you before, like hiding purchases in the trunk of the car or the back of the closet. My mother-in-law confessed to hiding things she didn't want her husband or kids to know about in a freezer in the garage. I know how it feels to *have* to be the first one to the mailbox so you can hide a bill from your financial partner (aka your spouse).

Are you wondering how to get the debt gorilla off your back? One thing I've learned from families who have conquered their debt has more to do with common sense than numbers. As columnist Ann Landers once said, "The best things in life aren't things." Those who lead lives of fiscal responsibility take this truism to heart and make lifestyle changes to reflect their new mind-set. Ask yourself: *Are my priorities in order? Do my family and I spend more time having good, "old-fashioned" fun together or visiting the mall?*

Debt was once the plague of the young and inexperienced. However, many of those now approaching the supposed "golden years" of retirement are struggling to keep their heads above a sea of debt. According to a survey conducted by the Consumer Bankruptcy Project, individuals ages 45 to 54 are now more likely than those who are younger to file bankruptcy on a per capita basis. A decline in saving is partly to blame, but baby-boomer bankruptcies are also caused by increasing medical costs, a lackluster job market, and the fact that many shoulder the double whammy of financial responsibility for their children and for aging parents.[1] You can avoid becoming a similar statistic by minimizing the amount of debt you owe at any given time.

Where to Start

All the money matters we've covered so far have led up to this discussion about debt, because you can never enjoy true financial security without getting your debt down to a reasonable level. There's no easy way to say this: if you're serious about reducing your debt, you must commit to spending money only on necessities as dictated by your budget. Having your priorities straight can ease the pain of focusing on just needs instead of wants. As a reminder, make a list of the top ten nonmaterial things for which you are thankful, and post the list where you'll see it often.

You got into debt by spending more than you make; the only way to get out of debt is by making more than you spend. Don't let credit fund a lifestyle you can't afford. Get spending under control by using cash or checks to pay for everything . . . no credit cards (cut them up if you must). Dedicate any lump-sum payments you receive, like bonuses or tax refunds, to paying down debt instead of to additional spending.

With respect to personal finances, not all bills are created equal. If it comes down to choosing what bills to pay first, follow this order to protect your assets: mortgage or rent, utilities, secured debts, credit cards and other unsecured debts, and medical bills. It's tempting to pay off smaller bills right away so you'll have fewer things to worry about. However, those with room in their budget for additional debt reduction, beyond regular monthly bills, should make extra payments above the minimum amount on debt with the highest interest rate (like credit cards). By focusing first on higher-interest debt, you'll free up more money faster for other purposes.

After paying off the balance on the card with the highest rate, add that monthly payment amount to what you are already paying on the card with the next highest interest rate, and so on. As you pay off each card, be sure to call the company and ask that it be canceled. Make a celebration out of cutting up the card—you've just lightened your financial load!

Although you don't want to deplete your emergency or retirement savings account, it's entirely reasonable to use some of your savings to pay debt down. (Remember to keep three to eight times your monthly salary available in an emergency fund.) Over time, the return on any investment is likely to be lower than the amount you're paying on high-rate debt. If you are paying 18 percent on credit card debt, but only earning 3 percent on extra money in your savings account, the debt is canceling out your savings because the rate is so much higher. As long as your job situation is not in jeopardy, trading off a little security now for the ability to save more money in the long run makes good sense.

Repayment through Refinancing

Refinancing any high-interest loan reduces your monthly payment and makes more cash available to pay down debt.

Credit cards. Probably the easiest way to get a lower interest rate on credit card debt is simply to ask. That's right, many times a simple phone call to the company will net you a reduction in your interest rate. If that doesn't work, consider moving your balance onto a card with a low rate on balance transfers. Just make sure that no fee will be charged for the transfer and that the rate after the introductory period is still lower than what you're paying now. A debt consolidation loan is a third option—you'll often pay a much lower rate on such a loan from a bank, especially if it is secured by a second mortgage on your home (which may also result in tax savings). Whichever option works for you, remember: the money freed up with lower payments should be used to further reduce debt, not to buy more stuff.

Vehicles. Before refinancing, check the loan documents on your existing car loan to make sure there are no prepayment penalties; then shop around for the lowest application fee and interest rate available. You will substantially cut the time it takes to pay off your new loan by continuing to pay the same, larger monthly amount as you paid on the original loan. Conversely, if you stretch out the term of the debt on your car and pay only the new lower amount, you will end up paying more in total interest even if your interest rate declined significantly.

Mortgages. When should you consider refinancing your mortgage? The majority of homeowners refinance their homes every two to five years due to moving, consolidating debt, or making home improvements. Even if these situations don't apply to you, there is a general rule of thumb for making the decision to refinance—if you can get a rate at least one percentage point lower than your existing mortgage rate and plan to keep the new mortgage for several years or more, then look at refinancing.

The amount of fees (or *closing costs*) you will pay for your new loan also affects the economics of refinancing. While it's essential to keep the amount of your monthly payments reasonable, minimizing interest costs and loan fees is equally important. Shop around for the lowest combination of interest rate and fees that will give you an affordable monthly payment. If you can recover the amount you'll have to spend in fees within one to two years as a result of your lower mortgage payments, it's usually a good idea to refinance. Here are some typical fees borrowers pay on new mortgages and refinanced loans:

- **Points** are fees the mortgage company charges for your loan. One point equals 1 percent of the mortgage amount. For example, one point on a $100,000 loan would be $1,000.
- An **appraisal** is an independent valuation of your property. Most companies will give you the names of appraisers whom they prefer you contact. Typical cost: $200–$400.
- **Title fees** are paid to a title company for searching to make sure there are no liens (money owed) on the property and legally recording the new mortgage. Typical cost: $125.
- **Title insurance** assures the company making the loan that the title is "clear." Typical cost for refinancing: $.04 per $1,000 of your mortgage amount. In other words, a $100,000 loan will cost you $400. The cost

is lower if this is a new mortgage because you share the expense with the seller.

- A new lender may ask for a **survey** of your property to verify its legal boundaries. Typical cost: $200–$300.
- You may incur **inspection fees** for termites, electrical and plumbing soundness, and a septic system (if you have one). Some companies will do all inspections for one flat fee of $200–$400.

Ask the mortgage company for an estimate of closing costs early so you can decide if refinancing makes sense. The company should provide you with the estimate within three days of your submitting an application *and all other required information*. Closing costs vary widely depending on the company you consult and the type of mortgage you request, but if it costs $4,000 to $5,000 to restructure a loan, it's hard to justify refinancing!

There are three main types of mortgage loans and about a million variations:

1. Fixed-rate, 30–year mortgage—With this mortgage, your interest rate and monthly payment amount remain basically the same for the next thirty years. If you plan to stay in your home for at least seven to ten years and rates are low, this is the mortgage for you.
2. Variable-rate, 30–year mortgage—The interest rate and monthly payment amount on this type of loan usually change every year for the next thirty years. An index (generally the "prime rate" of interest) is

used to determine the interest rate of your loan. The interest rate is bound by an upper and lower limit called a *ceiling* and a *floor* and is usually allowed to change only a few percentage points a year.

3. Adjustable-rate, 30–year mortgage—Adjustable-rate mortgages (ARMs) have similarities to both fixed- and variable-rate loans. The interest rate and payment amount can be fixed for five to seven years. At the end of this term, the interest rate is adjusted based on current rates, and then it stays the same for the remainder of the thirty-year term. Families planning to move before the adjustment date can usually count on a more consistent interest rate on their loan than with a variable rate and a lower rate than with a fixed-rate mortgage. If you stay in your home longer, ARMs are still better than fixed-rate mortgages if interest rates remain stable or fall until the time for your interest rate to be adjusted, because the rate usually starts out lower and automatically changes downward on the adjustment date without the costs associated with refinancing. If rates go higher by the adjustment date, you'll still have an advantage over refinancing at that time, because the new interest rate will be the same or lower than current rates to refinance, and you won't have to pay additional closing costs.

For the lowest closing costs and interest rates, consider a fifteen-year mortgage instead of a thirty-year loan. Your payments will be higher, but your loan balance declines much more quickly, and home equity builds faster. Even without a fifteen-year mortgage, you can shave years and thousands of dollars in interest off your loan by paying half your mortgage amount twice a month or simply adding an extra $20 or $50 to your regular mortgage payment. For most loans, each payment you make is divided between loan principal and interest, so paying more frequently or adding money to a payment reduces interest expense by paying down your loan balance more rapidly. Check your loan documents or call the mortgage company to make sure they allow you to prepay or make bimonthly payments before altering your payment schedule or amount. Some mortgage lenders will set up payment schedules specifically for bimonthly payments.

An alternative to refinancing is to ask your lender for a loan modification. Requesting a change to your payment amount, interest rate, or maturity date constitutes a loan modification. With this option, you don't have to complete new applications or loan documents, which lowers fees, particularly on home loans. In the case of asking for a reduced interest rate, your payments will be reduced, but the maturity date remains the same. If you purchased your home five years ago with a thirty-year mortgage, you will still have twenty-five more years to pay. Compare this with refinancing, where the time to pay off the loan goes back to thirty years again. Unfortunately, many times your original lender cannot agree to a modification because they have sold your loan to someone else. (Don't panic; this is a common practice in the mortgage industry.)

Using just one of the tactics we've discussed may not be enough to pare down your debt. Some friends of ours have greatly improved their financial situation with an assault on debt from two fronts. First, they refinanced their mortgage to lower their interest rate and consolidate credit card debt. Then, bonus and tax-return money was directly applied toward remaining credit card debt and an auto loan. These reductions lowered their overall monthly payments, as well as their total debt, to a manageable level.

Scaling Down

In the next chapter we'll look at practical and creative ways to save money. While these tips can save you hundreds of dollars over the course of a year, most families overlook a simple way to decrease the biggest debt producers: the concept of scaling down. By trading in your car for a less-expensive or older model, or selling your house and scaling down to a smaller one, you'll save thousands of dollars.

Soon after getting out of school and entering the workforce, I followed the crowd and bought a sporty new car. It had a great stereo and a sun roof and five-on-the-floor. I had a long commute to work every day, so my car and I were pretty close. When my husband and I began planning for my eventual transition from bank officer to stay-at-home mom, payments on the sporty car didn't fit into the new budget. (In retrospect, I don't think a baby car seat would have fit into the car either!) Selling that car and scaling down to an economy model was a tough choice, but with the lower payments, my new car was paid off in eighteen months, while I still would have been paying on the sporty car for another three years.

When families decide to buy a house, they often look at the purchase as part homestead, part investment. It's easy to get caught up in a real estate agent's encouragement to "buy the most home you can afford" and forget to ask yourself, "What will I be giving up to pay for such an expensive house?" Will you still be able to contribute to a retirement plan and put away money for the kids' college education? Can you set aside money to pay for things around the house that need updating or replacing? While home ownership has historically yielded good returns and allowed families to increase their net worth, a too-expensive home can stretch finances to the breaking point. Perhaps a house with less square footage or fewer amenities would satisfy your growing pains and allow you to reach other financial goals as well.

No doubt about it, these types of decisions are hard to make. Most often our pride prevents us from considering scaling down: pride in accomplishment and pride in ownership. In our upwardly mobile society, we often equate taking a step back with failure. But who is the real failure, the one who has everything she needs thanks to a willingness to scale down, or the one who loses everything for the sake of keeping up appearances? Only you can choose if a temporary step back now is worth financial security later.

Open Communication

Even though it's hard to do, talk to creditors before you fall far enough behind on payments that they call you. Most people avoid making the call due to embarrassment or because they think things will get better and they will catch up. But most creditors will work with you, including revising your payment schedule, if you call and explain the current situation (especially in the case of emergencies like a job loss or major illness). Secured creditors do not want to take possession of collateral on your debt, because they often do not earn enough from selling the collateral to cover the debt and related expenses. Unsecured creditors have an even greater interest in working out an arrangement with you, because they have no other way to get repaid.

Open communication also helps you avoid the legal fees creditors can add onto your balance if they have to take legal action. Waiting until you get three payments behind may mean you're too late to work out an arrangement with your lender that allows you to keep your car or home. And if you end up going to court, your wages may be *garnished*, which means your employer must deduct debt payments from your paycheck. The amount garnished could be more than you would have to pay now to catch your loan up. My husband makes a point of telling his new customers, "Please call me if you're going to be unable to make your payments. I'm a lot more understanding when I know what's going on." If you do make the call and negotiate a new payment schedule, ask your lender to send the new terms in writing to avoid any future misunderstandings.

Credit Counselors

Credit counselors provide information and one-on-one counseling sessions for those needing to improve their fiscal fitness. By first focusing on financial education and money management, reputable agencies work with you on a budget plan and then assess whether or not you need to enroll in a Debt Management Plan (DMP) for help with creditors. About one-third of agencies' clients are able to get debt down on their own through budgeting and lifestyle changes.

If you want to use the services of a credit counselor, look for a nonprofit agency that provides help for a nominal fee or free of charge. Many of these organizations are partially funded by the same credit industry that made it so easy for those with credit card debt to get where they are today! The National Foundation for Credit Counseling is a network of agencies providing services under the name Consumer Credit Counseling Service (CCCS), among others. You can visit their website at www.nfcc.org or call 1-800-388-2227 to find an office near you.

Credit counseling agencies may also negotiate with creditors to get payments down to a manageable level. With a Debt Management Plan, the credit counselor acts as an intermediary to negotiate with creditors for lower payments, reduced interest rates, and fee waivers. This enables clients to develop a payment plan that works for their income level. You then make one payment to the counseling agency, which distributes the payment to creditors according to an agreed-upon schedule. Before agreeing to a DMP, make sure you can afford the monthly payment; then contact your creditors to confirm that they have accepted the proposed plan.

Many private groups, using similar names and charging high fees, advertise that they can arrange for your unsecured debt to be paid off for a fraction of the real balance owed. These you want to avoid. The Federal Trade Commission (FTC) warns you to beware of credit repair companies that

- Guarantee they can remove your unsecured debt
- Promise that unsecured debts can be paid off with pennies on the dollar
- Claim that using their system will let you avoid bankruptcy
- Require substantial monthly service fees
- Demand payment of a percentage of savings
- Tell you to stop making payments to or communicating with your creditors
- Claim that creditors never sue consumers for nonpayment of unsecured debt
- Promise that using their system will have no negative impact on your credit report
- Claim that they can remove accurate, negative information from your credit report[2]

Bankruptcy

Even though the stigma of bankruptcy has waned significantly during the past decade, this choice should be your last resort. A bankruptcy filing remains on your credit report for ten years and results in the inability to obtain any kind of credit for at least the first two years—no car loans, home loans, or credit cards. If your car kicks the bucket, there's no way to buy a new one without paying a ridiculous rate of interest to a car-title lender. The only way to get a reasonable loan during this time would be to have mom, dad, or another adult with good credit cosign on the loan with you.

Still, some people struggling with debt have no choice but to file for bankruptcy. But bankruptcy does not make all debt problems go away. For example, the IRS will still hunt you down for any taxes you owe, and declaring bankruptcy does nothing to cure the underlying cause of overwhelming debt. Without learning how to manage money matters more responsibly, it's possible to have another gorilla on your back in no time.

On the plus side, all your nagging unsecured debt, like credit cards and medical bills, will disappear. For this reason, individuals are only allowed to declare bankruptcy once every seven years. You may *reaffirm*, or agree to continue to pay, the loans on assets you want to keep, like your home and autos. The lender must approve this arrangement but will only agree to do so if you keep payments current.

Mom's Money Makeovers

"It is easier to suppress the first desire, than to satisfy all that follow it," wrote Benjamin Franklin.[3] Self-denial is the price you must eventually pay for *not* keeping your desires under control. Getting debt down takes time and discipline, but the payoff is priceless: you'll have peace of mind.

At one time or another, getting debt down becomes an issue for most families. Pull out statements on any debt you owe, and make a table showing total debt amount, interest rate, and monthly payment amount. Then make a few phone calls to local banks or credit unions, and ask about current interest rates for different types of loans. This information will direct you toward your next step, whether that's refinancing, consolidating debt, or simply working through your current debt structure.

Frugal Family Financiers and Capable Currency Managers. Don't forget to take advantage of decreases in home-loan rates. Even though you may crave the consistency of a fixed-rate mortgage, an adjustable- or variable-rate mortgage can save you a lot of money in a stable or declining interest-rate environment, especially if you'll only be staying in your house for a few years.

Ambitious Breakeven Caretakers. The financial advice and materials provided by a credit counseling service can help you apply sound money management skills to start getting debt down. As an alternative, financial professionals like your local banker may be willing to sit down with you and work out a debt-reduction plan at no cost. Don't be afraid to put your financial security ahead of your pride and ask for help before you reach the financial point of no return.

Extravagant Home Economists. Can't get that gorilla off your back? If you have examined your priorities and made lifestyle changes on your own and still are unable to pay your bills and make ends meet, you may need the professional help of a credit counselor to establish a Debt Management Plan. A good credit counselor should also advise you on other options available if he or she is unable to help. Avoid the temptation to call the number of a "debt specialist" you've seen on TV. Instead, research the location of a CCCS office near you.

save big, save small 9

Downsizing has a negative connotation these days because it's most often associated with job loss, but what about downsizing our lifestyles? As consumers we worry about the price of new purchases, but we rarely take into consideration hidden costs like the energy used to produce them and additional space needed at home to hold them. Families purchase larger homes, which cost more to heat, cool, and care for, not just to accommodate more people, but to hold all their extra "stuff." We buy bigger cars for comfort and status and pay an exorbitant amount to fill them with gas. The ability to downsize, to base your lifestyle on what you need and can afford instead of keeping up with "the Joneses," is the first indication that you're recovering from See it, Want it, Buy it syndrome.

You can cut down on household expenses and clutter by considering three words before making a purchase—simplify, substitute, and share:

- *Simplify.* Do I really need this item?
- *Substitute.* Can I get something else that costs less? Can I make it myself?
- *Share.* Can I borrow this item? Would someone else agree to split the cost?

If there's something moms enjoy almost as much as saving money, it's sharing *how* they saved money. This chapter is devoted to the best money-saving tips from moms around the country. Suggestions range from specific how-tos of saving to general advice like this pearl of wisdom: "A one-dollar purchase is *not* a good bargain, if you do not need it."

General Money Savers

1. There are times of the year when certain items are less expensive. Shop off season, and save yourself a bundle.

January:	Christmas decorations, cards, and wrapping; winter clothing; workout and sports gear; televisions; bedding; computers
February:	housewares and small appliances; furniture; jewelry; chocolates
March:	outerwear; gardening supplies; luggage
April:	wallpaper and paint; china; men's and boys' suits
May:	major appliances; preseason sales on swimsuits and sandals

June: home furnishings; automobile tires; home-improvement tools and materials

July: major appliances; air conditioners; summer clothing; barbecue grills and supplies; radios and stereo equipment

August: bedding; outdoor furniture; school supplies; winter coats; back-to-school clothes

September: homes; bicycles; gardening supplies

October: cars; outdoor sports equipment; men's and boys' clothes

November: blankets and comforters; holiday meal fixings; fall clothing sales and winter markdowns

December: jewelry; ties; sweaters; perfume; popular gift items; food serving pieces; nursery and baby supplies

2. Let your fingers do the walking when you're looking for something specific. Calling stores and asking for pricing saves time, money, and gasoline for your car.

3. If you need to save money to catch up on bills, or just to get a little ahead, declare a "no spending" month, when you only pay bills and buy necessities like food, diapers, and gas—no toys, books, haircuts, movie rentals, clothes, or eating out. You'll be amazed how much you save.

4. Take to heart the notion, "It's the thought that counts." In gift giving, be more creative than extravagant.

5. Challenge your property tax bill if you think it's too high.

6. Keep nonperishable snacks and drinks in the car to cut down on visits to convenience stores and vending machines.

7. Ask for generic versions of the drugs your physician prescribes, which are much cheaper than brand names. (An exception: if the generic tastes worse than the brand name and your child refuses to take it, pay for the more-expensive medicine.)

8. Call and ask for your name to be removed from catalog mailing lists to cut back on the temptation to buy.

Housework

1. Use a hand towel, mop, and old rags instead of disposables like paper towels and cleaning wipes.

2. Pay less for cleaning products bought in bulk at an industrial cleaning supply store. Be sure to lock away extra cleaners out of the reach of small hands.

3. The markup on household cleaning products is huge, so consider making your own household cleansers. An excellent how-to book on the subject of nontoxic, homemade cleansers is *Clean and Green* by Annie Berthold-Bond.

Groceries

1. Always check grocery-store ads, paying special attention to "buy one, get one free" or "10 items for $10." If you can't use all of the products, share with a neighbor or freeze extras.
2. To coupon, or not to coupon, that is the question. Certainly don't use a coupon to buy an item you wouldn't ordinarily purchase. If you don't receive coupons in the Sunday newspaper, many are now available online. At sites like www.coolsavings.com, www.flamingoworld.com, and www.mycoupons.com, you can download coupons for groceries and baby, pet, and beauty products, to name a few. Many manufacturer websites have printable coupons too; look for web addresses on product packaging. To get coupons for your local store, visit www.valupage.com, enter your zip code, and choose a store in your area.

   There are downsides to online coupons. First of all, the sites where you find coupons usually request personal information in exchange—something we talked about avoiding in the earlier chapter about identity theft. As a consequence of the exchange, you may be inundated with unsolicited email messages and postal junk mail. There is also a danger that some online coupons are counterfeit, so don't waste time on offers that sound too good to be true.
3. Write out a list before you go, and *stick to it!*
4. Plan a month's worth of menus, and cook in bulk.

5. Don't buy food at a warehouse club that you're not going to use. Buying more than you need is wasteful regardless of how low the price. Consider dividing bulk goods, and their cost, among friends and neighbors.

6. Make large batches of convenience foods, like waffles, French toast sticks, and pancakes, in your own kitchen and freeze them. The food is still convenient when you want it and a lot less expensive.

7. Incorporate fruits and vegetables that are in season into your meal plan. For example, don't make strawberry shortcake in December—try apple crisp instead!

8. Buy steaks in the winter when no one's barbecuing and roasts in the summer when everyone tries not to use the oven.

9. Make less-expensive cuts of meat, like flank steak and chuck roast, tender by marinating overnight or cooking in the crock-pot.

10. Frozen fruits and vegetables are as nutritious as fresh ones and cheaper when that kind of produce is out of season.

11. Check per-unit costs before buying a larger size. Economy sizes are not always the best value.

12. The best deals on grocery-store aisles are on the top and bottom shelves. Manufacturers pay a premium to display their goods at eye level and pass the cost on to you.

13. Buy bread, rolls, and snack cakes from a bread or bakery outlet.

14. Serve breakfast, like huevos rancheros, once a week for dinner, or use meat as a garnish instead of the focus of a meal.

15. Purchase nonfood items at a discount store instead of the grocery store.

16. Frozen dinners are more expensive than homemade meals but cheaper than take-out food. Keep a few meals in the freezer for days when you don't have time to cook.

17. Only use individual drink boxes and bottles for lunches and picnics. Per pint, they cost much more than half-gallon cartons of juice or milk.

Gasoline and Utilities

1. Save money on gasoline (and car-repair expenses) by keeping your engine tuned and your tires inflated to their proper pressure.

2. Use your cruise control to get better gas mileage.

3. To save on electricity, make sure any new appliances, like air conditioners and furnaces, are energy efficient. Look for products that have earned the Energy Star logo from the Department of Energy and the Environmental Protection Agency. (It's a star next to the word "energy.")

4. Cut down on optional telephone services like caller ID and call waiting if it will save you money.

5. If you have a cell phone with free long-distance minutes, be sure to use those up before calling from your home phone.

6. Keep your dial-up Internet connection, even though it's slower, instead of switching to cable delivery or a DSL connection.

7. Do you really need all the extra channels offered by satellite and cable TV? If network programming suits you fine, downsize to an inexpensive basic package.

8. When lightbulbs burn out, replace them with compact fluorescent bulbs. They're more expensive than regular bulbs but use only 20 percent of the power and have an estimated five-year life span. Some utility companies even offer rebates on the cost of fluorescent bulbs.

9. Turn off electronic devices, like your cable box, TV, or computer, instead of leaving them on in standby mode.

10. Train everyone in the house to turn off lights, fans, radios, TVs, and other appliances when not in use.

11. Setting the washing machine's water-temperature dial on cold, or warm with a cold rinse, saves energy.

12. Turn the temperature on your hot water heater down to 120 degrees to save energy and prevent hot water scalding.

13. It takes more energy to keep a freezer cold when it's half empty. Try freezing water in used milk containers to fill up unused space.

14. If you're buying a new refrigerator, consider a top-freezer model, which uses less energy than side-by-sides.

15. Cover window air conditioners and ventilation fans during cold weather so more heat will stay in the house.

16. Clean or replace air filters on your cooling and heating systems every one or two months to increase efficiency.

Kids' Stuff

1. Register on the Internet with companies that make kids' stuff, like www.gerber.com, www.huggies.com, or www.pampers.com. These sites allow you to sign up for coupons on their products.

2. Remember that infants and young children have no label sensitivity (unless you instill it). You can save a lot during these years by using hand-me-downs or buying at secondhand stores and garage sales.

3. Use washcloths more often than paper towels or baby wipes, because you can throw them in the laundry and reuse.

4. Swap kids' toys and clothes with family, friends, and neighbors.

5. Buy used sporting goods and equipment for children on eBay or at a secondhand store like Play It Again Sports.

6. Use plain colors to decorate a child's room and accessorize with inexpensive posters, pillows, and wall hangings that are easily replaced to suit the child's changing tastes.

7. Contain playthings in baskets and hampers instead of plastic toy boxes that you'll want to replace as kids get older.

8. At birthday parties, ask everyone to bring a gift to exchange. You'll have fewer toys to find places for, and everyone goes home with a small gift instead of a goody bag.

9. If you are moving, or know someone who is, keep several large boxes to make into clubhouses, space stations, and castles. Kids can decorate the outsides with crayons or washable markers.

Entertainment

1. Dramatically cut the cost of going out by trading babysitting time with another family.

2. Try one of these low-cost date night ideas—just as much fun at less than half the price!

   • In an effort to cut down on the expense of going out, one mom spent an evening strolling through the local bookstore with her husband—only to find they couldn't resist the temptation to pick up an interesting read and enjoy a couple of cups of coffee in the café. Instead of visiting a literary megastore, find a local used bookstore and browse. You can pick out a "must have" book, go out for coffee, and still spend less than the cost of a new book.

(The same thing goes for music CDs.)

- Pack a blanket and a picnic dinner, and go out to the park.
- Attend a lecture on a subject of interest to both of you at your local library or community college.

3. Share season tickets to plays, a musical series, or sporting events with a friend or neighbor. It's even cheaper if you take turns babysitting on the nights the other couple is out on the town.
4. Do lunch instead of going out to dinner. Lunch menus are often less expensive.
5. Make good use of your library card for free books, audio CDs, movies, and books on tape.

Holidays and Special Occasions

1. Buy gifts throughout the year, whenever you see things on sale, and put them away until needed. Keep a running list of what you've bought and for whom, so you don't end up with three plaid throws for Uncle Bob.
2. When wrapping gifts, try to incorporate part of the gift as wrapping paper, like using a tea towel to wrap up kitchen goodies.
3. For holiday spending, set a budget equal to no more than 1 percent of your yearly income, or limit purchases to what you can afford without the use of credit cards or layaway plans.

4. During the holidays, write down credit card purchases in a small notebook kept in your purse to make sure you don't charge more than can be paid off at the end of the month.

5. If you plan to downsize holiday gift giving, talk to family members ahead of time. Focus on your desire to add meaning, as well as more time together, to your celebrations.

6. Ask family and close friends to accompany you on an outing instead of exchanging gifts. Visit a local holiday light exhibit together, and then invite them over for hot chocolate, cookies, and conversation.

7. Put together a theme basket of gifts for a family instead of individual presents—for example, a DVD movie, microwave popcorn, and drinks.

8. Split the cost of a large or special present between several family members.

9. Order a subscription to something that can be enjoyed throughout the year.

10. Give a gift certificate. If used at an after-Christmas sale, the recipient can pick out the perfect present and get much more for the money.

Monthly Expenses

1. Save money on insurance premiums by getting a policy with a higher deductible and putting the difference in a savings account until you have enough to pay for that deductible.

2. Some insurance companies charge fees for the convenience of making monthly premium payments. Cut costs by putting enough into a savings account each month to cover an annual or semiannual insurance bill instead.

3. If you typically carry a balance on your credit card, consider switching to one with a lower interest rate. (Be sure to cancel your old card!) Another option is to call your own card company and ask them to lower your rate.

4. Call your mortgage lender and find out the remaining balance in your escrow account (money the lender holds to pay your property taxes and insurance) after the year's expenses have been paid. If insurance costs and taxes have gone down or your lender has overestimated the amounts, you may be paying too much and have a surplus that can be refunded to you.

Major Purchases

1. Buy used for better value, especially with vehicles. Compare the seller's asking price with the average retail price in an updated *NADA Official Used Car Guide*, found at libraries, banks, and credit unions.

2. Banks and credit unions tend to offer better deals on used-car financing than other types of lenders, like finance companies or even car dealerships.

3. Investigate offers on new cars, like 0 percent financing or $2,000 cash back. Ask for the total amount of inter-

est you'll pay on a loan from the dealer if you take the rebate (deduct the cash back reward), and compare that against the interest you'd pay on a loan from your local bank including any fees. Then take the best deal.

4. To get the biggest increase in value over time on the purchase of a home, look for the smallest house available in the nicest area you can afford. You can enjoy the neighborhood amenities while your home appreciates along with the rest of the houses on your block.

5. Make an extra mortgage payment during the year, or add a little extra to your mortgage payment each month (check your loan documents to make sure you are allowed to prepay). If your budget can handle it, consider a mortgage loan where you make payments twice a month. All of these tips will save on interest expense and reduce your loan balance more quickly.

6. If you live in a stable neighborhood, share the cost of big ticket items, like a riding mower or snow and leaf blowers, with your neighbors.

7. Electronics, appliance, and furniture stores might give you a better deal than the posted price if you ask. They may honor another store's lower price advertisement, or you can ask if their price can be reduced by a percentage if you pay in cash. You certainly won't receive a discount without asking, yet you haven't lost a thing if the salesperson refuses.

8. Learn how to do simple home repairs and improvements yourself. Check books out from the library, or attend free seminars at home and hardware stores.

kids' money management   10

Young children have very little concept of the value of money. They tend to estimate the cost of an item based on how important it is to them. When asked, my children were just as likely to say their favorite candy bar cost $100 as the actual price of $1.

Not surprisingly, research shows that educating children about money makes a difference in their financial futures. People who don't end up learning about credit, borrowing, and interest as children are often unable to successfully manage financial affairs as adults. Kids graduating from schools in states that mandate personal-finance classes have higher savings rates and net worth than those in states without such courses. However, financial literacy is a lifelong process and not one that we can assign solely to our schools. After modeling responsible financial behavior, the next most important tool moms can use to improve children's financial literacy is to talk money together.

Many of us grew up with the impression that talking about money was impolite, but financial experts encourage us to be up-front with kids about the amount of money we make, as well as how much things cost. My own experience has shown that discretion should be applied in giving out financial information you would prefer not to share with the rest of the town. Our preschool son once shared with the teller at the bank—and the entire lobby as well—the fact that my husband's job had been "downsized." Another time I discovered that one of our children had bragged about our annual income at a church meeting—to one of the other kids. While kids can greatly benefit by sharing your financial struggles and successes, consider their understanding of confidentiality and discretion in choosing what information to share.

Do let kids in on your thought process when deciding whether or not to make a purchase. Verbalize the pros and cons, especially when you are saying no to something you really want but don't have in your budget. As with other life lessons, kids learn just as much from the negative experiences you impart as from positive ones. Telling them about your money mistakes and how you've recovered lets children know they are not "bad" if they run into financial problems of their own.

Kids absorb our attitudes toward finances, but they also watch what value friends and neighbors place on money and belongings. Dr. T. Berry Brazelton writes, "Money needs to be equated with responsibility: Responsibility for saving, for sharing with others, and for spending wisely. In our society that's not always the message that comes across. More often it's 'money equals power.'"[1]

We need to counteract negative influences so that our children will learn to be content with what they have. Instead of promoting competition, encourage cooperation by tackling family financial projects together. For example, show kids how savings multiply by having everyone empty their pennies into a large container at the end of each day. When the container is full, let family members take turns deciding how the funds should be spent. Several board games that involve the earning and spending (or losing) of play money have stood the test of time. Sit down and enjoy games of Monopoly, Monopoly Junior, or The Game of Life with your kids. To instill the notion that it's not always necessary to spend money in order to have a good time, be sure to balance free fun with activities that cost a modest amount during family times together.

Money should not be frightening. While children must learn that we have a limited quantity of money and therefore must choose what to do with it, constantly saying, "We can't afford that," makes kids fearful. Instead, stress that you want to have enough for the things you need. Try saying, "We don't choose to spend our money that way," or "That isn't in our budget." Emphasize that money is a means to an end, not the be-all and end-all.

Very Young Children

Starting when kids are very young, introduce them to the concept that they can't have everything they want. Learning the fine arts of delayed gratification and prioritizing will pay dividends for your child beyond simple money matters. Begin by offering everyday choices—food to eat, toys to play with—so children become accustomed to making trade-offs and leaving something behind.

Before shopping with your children, discuss what you plan to buy, and let them know there will be no spur-of-the-moment purchases. If children get a treat on every shopping trip, they come to expect it. Offer rewards for cooperative behavior, like a special snack at home or playing a game together after the trip. At the store, point out how you pay for things before taking them home. To make this example most effective, pay with cash. At home your child can play store without handling real money if you cut oversized green rectangles and brown circles out of construction paper and use them as play money.

Preschoolers

During the preschool years, kids should learn that money doesn't grow on trees—mom and dad get paid for work they do and use that money to buy things for the family. ATMs, which magically spit out cash, create a lot of confusion for children on this point. Ideally your preschooler should occasionally observe bank transactions when you hand a check to a real, live teller and receive cash in return. When using an ATM, explain that you are able to get money out because you first worked in order for it to be put in (this same explanation applies for withdrawing funds from the bank).

Once your children reach age three, they can begin to handle all kinds of money (remind them not to put coins in their mouths). Use these play concepts as tools to teach your children about money mechanics:

- Place a collection of coins on a table and have your child sort them. Talk about the names of the coins.
- Make coin rubbings by placing paper over coins and rubbing the flat side of a crayon over them. Can your child identify coins from the rubbings?
- Set up a make-believe store and take turns playing shopper and sales clerk. Label items with prices, starting with just pennies. Slowly add new coin denominations, changing the prices each time. Help your child choose the correct coins to pay.
- Tape real coins to three-by-five-inch index cards. Make sure you have two cards for each type or combination of coins. Turn the cards over, mix them up, and play a game of Concentration.
- Give your child enough money to purchase a snack or drink, and help him or her go through the process of paying the cashier, explaining each step as you go. If your child picks out something too expensive, explain the need to choose something that's affordable.

Monitor the amount of time your child spends in front of the television and all those commercials. I knew our youngest son had been watching too much TV when we pulled into the parking lot of a home-improvement store and he began singing the store's advertising jingle! Choose noncommercial channels and programs on DVD when possible.

Elementary and Middle School Age

This is the time to introduce denominations of paper money and to give your child lots of practice making change. While working at a softball concession stand, I noticed how inexperienced my children, along with many of the other cashiers, were at figuring change due. The majority of items were not priced in multiples of ten cents; for example, hot dogs cost $1.25 and candy was $.65. Kids of all ages had such a tough time adding up purchases and giving back change that we supplied a calculator to cut back on losses from cashier mistakes!

At this age kids really begin to feel pressure to conform, and often that translates into shopping and spending. Balance peer pressure with activities that promote your own values, like volunteering, spending time outdoors, reading a library book aloud, or playing sports. The value of saving can also be learned. Here are six simple ways to encourage your child to be a super saver:

1. Talk your children through your trips to the grocery store. Let your children see how coupons help save money.
2. Teach kids how to comparison shop between similar items of different sizes and prices.

3. Help younger children focus on savings goals by hanging a picture of what they want to buy on the refrigerator.

4. Encourage delayed gratification by suggesting kids ask for nonessential items for birthday or holiday gifts rather than buy these items immediately.

5. Help your children make a list of the five things they would most like to buy, and assign a price to each so they can set up savings goals.

6. Offer encouragement for your children's efforts. When they reach their goal, take them shopping promptly as a reward.

Another way to teach the virtues of thriftiness is by opening a savings account together in your child's name; you can be a cosigner on the account. Our community bank offers a program at the grade school where kids can make weekly deposits into a savings account of their own. Monthly savings account fees are waived so students get to keep all their savings and interest. The bank awards prizes at the end of the year for all savers, with special recognitions to those who make a deposit, however small, every week. This program also provides an opportunity to teach kids how money grows by earning interest and to dispel some misconceptions about the way a bank works. For example, the youngest savers often believe that the bank puts their dollar bill in a specific place in the vault, so they can withdraw that very same dollar at a later date.

School-age children readily embrace spending and grudg-ingly accept the concept of saving, but they may be a bit fuzzy on the need to give. Let kids "catch" you being gen-erous with others and sharing what you have. Find out for yourself which charities your church supports; then openly discuss what happens to the money you put in the collection plate. Even exposing kids to everyday acts of kindness, like buying food to take to a family who has experienced a birth or a death, helps make the needs of others more real.

Allowances are discussed separately in the following sec-tion, but whether or not you choose to give allowances and irrespective of whether they are tied to household chores, kids should be offered extra tasks they can perform to earn additional spending money. This gives children real-world experience with working for pay and provides positive re-inforcement of their budding work ethic.

Allowances

In chapter 5, "'Lay' a Nest Egg," I talked about how savings rates in this country have dramatically declined. Becoming a spender society may be due, in part, to the demise in many families of the tradition of *allowances*. At our house, allowances are a measure of our children's growth and development, but an informal poll of my girlfriends revealed that we are the only family in our circle of friends that continues this tradition. Paying an allowance is one way to avoid having kids constantly come to you for a handout, and allowances help teach them how to make choices about spending and saving their own money.

Financial experts usually suggest that parents begin paying allowances around age five or six. The start of an allowance should also herald the beginning of saving and giving. As with your own income, your child should set aside money for these purposes first and only spend what's left. Empty plastic jars labeled "Giving," "Saving," and "Spending" make good banks because your child can watch his or her money accumulate.

How much should kids receive as an allowance? They need enough to divide into their banks for various goals, while leaving an amount in spending that allows small consumers to make reasonable purchases. One suggestion is to give a dollar for each year of your child's age. However, several other factors should help determine the actual amount, including the effect an allowance will have on your budget, the "going rate" received by friends, and what financial responsibilities you expect a child to shoulder. Take the time to sit down together and discuss what should be paid for out of the allowance—write it down, and post the list in a conspicuous place if your child is prone to overspend. This tactic will save you from endless arguing and wheedling later.

One of the biggest questions about allowances is whether they should be based on helping around the house. We've always followed the policy that kids do a share of the work because they're part of the family. If they don't finish their chores, we assess a consequence other than losing their allowance (like having a privilege revoked). Some families believe that allowances should be earned—each chore kids successfully complete is worth a predetermined amount. Others believe that children start out with an allowance and deductions are made for misbehavior. An infinite number of possible scenarios exist. To institute an allowance program, consider which arrangement best suits your values and your pocketbook, but avoid turning allowances into a power struggle.

When paying allowances, give kids sufficient change so that the money can be easily divided. For example, instead of handing over a one-dollar bill, give three quarters, two dimes, and a nickel. (Allocate 10 percent into savings, 10 percent for giving, and 80 percent to spend, or any other combination you and your child have chosen.) Consistency is also very important. Think how difficult it would be for you to budget and save if you couldn't count on receiving your paycheck from one week to the next! Although you may establish guidelines for how your budding financiers spend their money, let your children make some of their own mistakes. A child will learn much more about truth in advertising and quality of workmanship through one poor purchase than through any amount of lecturing.

Teenagers

Kids this age need to understand that paying for necessities comes before the purchase of any "wants." To visually demonstrate how this works, cash in your next paycheck;

then have your teen help divide up the money between bills that must be paid. Count up what's left, and discuss how the remainder could be used. This exercise provides many teenagers with a much-needed reality check.

Teens should also be able to put the basics of budgeting into practice. Consider paying their allowances on a bi-weekly basis to increase awareness of money management in the working world. Even kids who enjoy dressing down care about their clothes, so another way to introduce budgeting is with a clothing allowance. Label-sensitive teens can learn to compensate for those "must-have" designer jeans or tennis shoes by shopping at discount stores for other items. If you require that teens contribute their own spending money to cover budget shortfalls, they may think twice about the importance of a logo. If your child frequently runs out of funds, give him or her a notebook to record every purchase. This is a good activity for any money management personality, because it allows kids to tangibly keep track of how they spend their money.

Managing a checking account is one of the new skills teenagers can undertake. Make sure they understand the basics, including service charges and overdraft fees, before handing them a checkbook. Resist the temptation to bail your children out if they run out of money, so that they won't expect handouts later. If your teen does come to you with a reasonable request for a loan, charge him or her interest, and set a firm date for repayment.

On the flip side, regardless of how much we've given our kids, they take exception to us using them as an ATM in a pinch. If you do borrow from your children, be sure to pay them back promptly with interest. Teenagers still watch how we manage our own finances, so modeling the behavior we expect from them helps avoid complaints of "that's not fair."

Give a credit card to your teenager? "No way," many moms would respond. Depending on the level of responsibility and maturity exhibited by your teen, it may be time to rethink the credit card ban. By the time your child is an adult, he or she may actually live in a nearly paperless society where paying with plastic is required. The sooner teens learn about credit cards and how to use them responsibly, the better prepared they will be for the future.

There are a few ways to give your teens credit experience without allowing them to run up big debts. One approach is to allow your child to be a "user" on your credit card so you can monitor how much he or she spends. You may also help him or her get a secured credit card—the type of card tied to a deposit account where the credit limit equals the amount deposited. To provide experience with plastic without the risk of credit, let your teens apply for a debit card for their checking accounts, or provide them with a prepaid credit card. With these two options, kids can't spend more than the cash that's available.

Before handing over any type of card, sit down with your teen, and set a limit for the amount he or she can charge each month. Kids also need to understand that, from the first charge they make to a credit card in their name, credit bureaus will begin maintaining a credit report that can be reviewed by potential employers, lenders, insurance companies, and apartment managers.

Upon leaving home, many kids operate under the misconception that they will continue to live at the same socioeconomic level as you have provided. Many kids today enter the workforce with a sense of entitlement and a distinct lack of interest in working their way up the financial ladder. Can your children differentiate between "wants" and true "needs"? Don't send them out unprepared. Encourage financial independence by educating teenagers about the cost of everyday needs and the work it takes to cover those costs. Discuss various careers and the education they require, and do some research to learn about starting salaries.

Financial Literacy Online

On these websites, kids and adults can play games, take interactive lessons, and test their knowledge about various financial topics:

- National Council on Economic Education
  www.ncee.net
- Jump$tart Coalition for Personal Financial Literacy
  www.jumpstart.org
- U.S. Treasury Department
  www.treas.gov/kids/
- Federal Reserve
  www.federalreserveeducation.org

In talking with your children about money, you'll probably discover that they already know more than you would expect due to their own observations. Since the way we manage our money reflects some of our deepest family values, these skills should not be left to the TV, our children's friends, or "the Joneses." Like those discussions about the birds and the bees, money matters are best taught by parents. Anyone for a game of Monopoly?

Mom's Money Makeovers

Kids have money management personalities just as we do. Although our modeling and instruction influence their understanding of finances, you may notice one child hoarding her allowance while another's burns a hole in his pocket. Use what you've learned about money management personalities to help your child enjoy fiscal responsibility.

Frugal Family Financiers. Encourage a child with hoarding tendencies to experience the satisfaction of buying something on his own. Offer to pay for part of something he wants, if your child will loosen the purse strings and make up the difference.

Capable Currency Managers. Help your child plan how to use her resources by brainstorming about the consequences of various actions. Let her think of the possible combinations of spending and saving, and talk about the future impact of the various options. If she buys a doll now, how will she feel when she has nothing left to spend on vacation?

Ambitious Breakeven Caretakers. If there's a spender in your house, make it easier for him to save by giving allowances on Sunday evening instead of Friday. He'll have to do a better job of budgeting for the busy weekend when it's a week away.

Extravagant Home Economists. Big spenders tend to be disorganized, which translates into fiscal irresponsibility. Older ones lose control of their finances; younger spenders just lose money. Help your child set aside a convenient place to keep her cash, and make sure the money gets put away until your child gets the hang of doing it herself.

moms' questions and answers   11

Moms in several MOPS (Mothers of Preschoolers) groups I visited graciously responded to a survey that asked, "If you could ask a financial expert any question, what would it be?" Here are the questions and answers not already discussed in other chapters.

How do you know the difference between wants and needs?

These can be difficult to define, because what constitutes a want or need may differ for everyone. In the strictest sense, we have very few needs—food (not including choice cuts of meat and cereal with the latest superhero's picture on the box), clean water (usually not bottled), clothes (without designer tags), and a roof over our heads (not the biggest and in the very best part of town). I would include medical and dental care on the list. What else do you *really* need?

If you start with this very short list, most everything else could be considered a "want." Take, for example, having two family cars. We don't really need both, not in the sense that our existence would be threatened without them. But with only one vehicle, my husband and I would have a very difficult time getting the kids to school (there's only limited bus service in our area) and all the other places they, and I, go. (Okay, we don't actually *need* to go as many places as we do either!)

Perhaps the best way to distinguish real needs from wants is with a two-pronged approach. *First, never buy anything impulsively.* If it's a small purchase, like a new outfit, sleep on it overnight, and see if you still want it enough the next day to go back and buy it. For larger purchases, like new appliances or vehicles, you should sleep on it a lot longer! *Second, never replace an item if you already have one that works.* The cheapest car, home, clothes, and washer and dryer are the ones you already have. The only caveat to this is if the item in question is about to wear out, you cannot satisfactorily fix it at a reasonable price, AND you've stumbled upon a great deal—then it's probably time for an upgrade.

How do you find the time to get finances in order?

I don't know anyone who *finds* the time for such an exciting endeavor (she says jokingly). If sound money management and building a financial future for your family are important, you will have to *make* the time for it to happen. Just like reorganizing your closets, drawers, and cabinets, straightening out your finances is a job you commit to undertake and then work at a little bit at a time. Don't try to do everything at once. If you are part of a couple, divide up the tasks described in chapter 3, "Get Control of Your Finances," and block out a couple of nights a week to sit down and work side by side at the kitchen table. I'm tempted to say, "Make it fun," but realistically, you can make the work less tedious by listening to music and making dessert to enjoy together.

How can I limit myself when I have "extra" money, instead of spending it on things that I don't really need?

Shopaholic tendencies are particularly strong in free-wheeling Extravagant Home Economists. The mom who asked this question went on to say that she has purchased more clothes on shopping binges than her kids can wear. Whenever you have extra money in your checking account, put it out of sight and out of mind by immediately transferring it to a savings account. Whether it's an emergency account, vacation account, retirement account, or education account is up to you. However, don't sabotage your savings efforts by being overly strict with yourself. Sometimes a trip to the discount store for something small can stave off a buying binge later.

Another possibility is to give each spouse a "blow fund" as a category in your budget. That way, when you have an impulse buy or want something you don't need, you can use that money, and it's already planned for. But you might be amazed at how reluctant you are to use that cash when it's piling up in the envelope and you know you could be saving for something big.

*I don't have the time to go to two or three different grocery
stores each week in order to hit the sales. Plus, it costs me
more in time and gasoline to get to some of the discount stores.
What's the best way to maximize savings on food expenses?*

Running from one store to the other often isn't worth
the small amount you save. As you visit different stores,
keep a price book that shows where to get the best deals
on the things you need. Choose only one or two stores to
visit each week, and stock up on enough nonperishable
items to hold you over until you are scheduled to go back
to that store. Shop the sales at the stores you do visit for
perishable foods like produce.

*How can I cut back on fast-food trips on the way to or from
kids' activities and while running errands?*

It's always cheaper to bring food from home than to eat
out on the road. Discount and kitchen stores carry plastic lunch containers with compartments, like Lunchables
meals from the grocery. Fill up these containers with fresh,
nutritious food before setting off on a trip that interferes
with a meal. To stave off the munchies during errands, keep
nonperishable snacks and drinks in the car.

*Do I need to buy life insurance for my children? If so,
how much should I get and what is the best age to start?*

Only consider life insurance for your children after you
have purchased enough life insurance for the adults in the
family. A child's policy should not be used for a college

fund or other investments—there are better ways to save money and make it grow (see chapter 5, "'Lay' a Nest Egg"). Children's life insurance is designed to pay for expenses in the event of their death. Adding a rider onto your own policy, or onto dad's, is the most cost-effective way to get this kind of coverage.

When you are self-employed, how do you handle budgeting and cash flow if the income from your home business varies from month to month?

Budgeting with variable income and expenses presents quite a challenge. If your income is higher during certain months of the year, following the "cross-training" budgeting technique—going through an entire year's deposits and payments (see chapter 3, "Get Control of Your Finances")—is the only way to come up with a budget that reasonably predicts your cash flow from month to month. When you don't have the safety net of a regular paycheck, an emergency fund where you've saved six to eight months' worth of take-home pay becomes even more important.

For those who have no idea when income will arrive, take the previous year's total income and expenses, and divide by twelve for monthly budget amounts. In the months when you are waiting for payments from customers, take the amount you need to meet your income budget out of your emergency fund. In months when you receive more than your budgeted income, deposit the extra back into the emergency fund.

Those who are self-employed also can run into problems obtaining financing, because they often show very little net income for tax purposes. Don't downplay your income to the point where a lender cannot reasonably make you a loan. Your best bet is to establish a relationship with a financial institution and ask what steps you should take to qualify for a loan.

How can you stop worrying about finances?

In his book *The First National Bank of Dad*, David Owen writes, "No one spends more time brooding about money than someone who is scared of it, or who doesn't understand it, or who willfully tries to ignore it."[1] It's natural to worry about money, but in the end there are really only three things you can do about your finances:

- Make more money by increasing paid working hours with a part-time job or home business, or by changing to a higher-income job.
- Spend less by preparing and sticking to a budget and practicing cost-cutting measures.
- Adjust your expectations so that you are satisfied spending less than you earn.

On my grandmother's ninety-fifth birthday, our family accompanied her to church. During the sermon, the speaker concluded with this simple yet profound observation: "A life richly lived is measured not by what belongs to you, but by to whom you belong." What an inspiration to both hear this wisdom and see it living in my grandmother. She has never been truly rich in belongings, and her time for the accumulation of things has passed. However, my grandmother's wealth, when measured by her faith, many friends, and cherished family, cannot be counted.

You've taken on the responsibility of educating yourself about money matters. It's time to transfer worry into action—use what you have learned to make positive changes in your fiscal fitness. Which of the three suggestions above makes the most sense for your family? Live richly by taking what steps you can toward financial security and, above all, by giving thanks to the one who gives us every good gift . . . the one to whom we truly belong.

glossary of everyday financial terms

Adjustable Rate—Interest rate that changes after a specified period of time.

Adverse Action Notice—Notice explaining why your loan request has been denied. It may offer an alternative that would make the loan acceptable.

APR—Annual Percentage Rate. Annual amount of interest you pay on a loan or earn on an investment.

APY—Annual Percentage Yield. Overall rate of return earned on an investment. The APY can be higher than the APR when the interest you earn on an investment also earns interest. (It's reinvested instead of paid out to you each month.)

Asset—Something you own that has value.

ATM—Automated Teller Machine.

Automatic Deduction (Automatic Debit)—Payment automatically made from your checking account based on an agreement you've signed with a company for services, like insurance, health club membership, or Internet service.

Budget—The process of setting limits on your spending. Also, a list of the amounts to which you want to hold expenditures on a weekly, monthly, or yearly basis for various expense categories, like food, clothing, utilities, and entertainment.

Cash Flow Statement—Shows the difference between the amount of cash you bring in each month (or year) and what you pay out in expenses.

Closing Costs—Fees and other expenses you must pay to buy a home or to refinance an existing home mortgage, which can include points, an appraisal fee, title fees, title insurance, a survey, and inspection fees.

Collateral—Asset you offer to a creditor in order to get a loan. The creditor has the right to sell the asset if you don't repay your debt.

Collection Action—When the original creditor hires a collection agency to collect the debt.

Commission—Fee earned by the person or company that sells you investment products. When a commission is charged for a mutual fund, it's called a _load_.

Credit—The ability to buy or use something and pay for it later.

Credit Line—A loan where the full amount doesn't have to be taken out at one time. The borrower has the right to request a portion of the line as needed.

Debit Card—Basically an electronic check. You use the card at a retailer or ATM, and the money is taken directly out of your checking account.

Debt Consolidation—Combining two or more debts together into one loan.

Direct Deposit—Money that is electronically deposited directly into your bank account.

Discretionary (Controllable) Expenses—Types of expenses that generally are "wants," not "needs." You decide how much to spend on them.

Diversification—Putting money in different kinds of investments to spread risk.

Equity—The money you would have left after selling an asset and paying off the debt you owe for originally purchasing the asset. (Example: the equity in your home is its value minus the mortgage amount against it.) Also, the increase in value of an asset since you bought it.

Expenses—What you pay for goods and services.

Fixed Expenses—Expenses with amounts that cannot easily be increased or decreased, like rent or car payments.

Fixed Rate—An interest rate that doesn't change for the term of a loan.

Foreclosure—Process by which a lender takes ownership of your property for nonpayment of the debt.

Home Equity Loan—Borrowing against the equity in your house. A loan secured by a mortgage against your home.

Income—Any kind of money you earn.

Inflation—The rate at which the average prices of goods and services increase from one year to the next.

Interest—Money paid to you, or by you to someone else, for the use of funds.

Investment—An asset you purchase with the hope it will increase in value.

Investment Portfolio—All the assets you've purchased taken together as a group.

Liability—What you owe for purchasing a good or service.

Loan Modification—Modifies the basic terms of an existing loan without refinancing (creating a new loan).

Maturity Date—Final date when the balance remaining on a loan is due, or the date when your investment pays off.

Minimum Balance Requirement—Amount of money you must keep in your bank account at all times to avoid fees.

Mortgage—Loan secured by your house or other real estate.

Net Worth—Your total assets (what you own) minus total debts (what you owe).

Overdraft Fee—Fee charged by the bank when a debit out of your account makes your account balance negative.

Prime Rate—The interest rate a lending institution offers its best customers.

Reaffirmation—An agreement between you and a lender, during a bankruptcy, that you will continue making payments.

Reconciliation—Making sure the amount in your checkbook register and the amount in your bank account are the same as of a certain date.

Refinancing—Creating a new loan to lower monthly payments, lower the interest rate, or extend the term of an existing loan or to borrow additional funds.

Risk Adverse—Someone unwilling to make investments with the possibility of losing his or her money.

Risk Threshold—The amount of risk you are willing to take with your investments. Beyond this point you become risk adverse.

Secured—A loan where collateral is pledged.

Term—Length of time to the maturity date of a loan or investment.

Time Horizon—Amount of time your investments have to grow in value before you will need the money.

Uniform Transfers to Minors Act—Allows parents and grandparents to transfer property to a child through a will or a gift, such that the property can only be used for the sole benefit of that child. The money or property is handled by a custodian (any adult), who is subject to criminal penalties if the money is not used for the benefit of the child. This helps protect your child's assets until he or she reaches the age of majority.

Unsecured—Loan in which no collateral (assets) are pledged.

Variable Rate—A loan rate tied to an economic index (like the prime rate), so that the rate fluctuates monthly, quarterly, semiannually, or yearly. The rate can go up or down, but usually there is a limit to how much it can change per year and over the life of the loan.

Wage Garnishment—A voluntary or involuntary direct deduction from your paycheck to repay debt.

notes

Introduction

1. Michael Moncur, The Quotations Page, 2004, http://www.quotationspage.com.
2. U. S. Department of Agriculture, "Consumer Expenditure Survey," 2003, http://www.usda.gov/cnpp/Crc/crc2003.pdf.

Chapter 1: Money 101

1. Quoted in Rosalie Maggio, *The New Beacon Book of Quotations by Women* (Boston: Beacon Press, 1996), 256.

Chapter 3: Get Control of Your Finances

1. Michael Moncur, The Quotations Page, 2004, http://www.quotationspage.com.

Chapter 5: "Lay" a Nest Egg

1. Michael Moncur, The Quotations Page, 2004, http://www.quotationspage.com.
2. Gini Kopecky Wallace, "Can Money Buy Happiness?", *Family Circle*, April 15, 2003, 65.
3. The College Board, "Annual Survey of Colleges," 2004, http://collegeboard.com/prod_downloads/press/cost04/041264TrendsPricing2004_FINAL.pdf.
4. "Medicare Seen Insolvent by 2019," March 23, 2004, http://www.cbsnews.com/stories/2004/03/23/politics/printable608201.shtml.

5. Morningstar, Inc., "Is Your Retirement Portfolio on Track?", Morningstar.com's Interactive Classroom, 2002, http://news.morningstar.com/classroom/print_quiz/0,3270,3234,00.html.

6. Federal Trade Commission, "FTC Charity Checklist," Federal Trade Commission—Facts for Consumers, May 2003, http://www.ftc.gov/bcp/conline/pubs/misc/charitycheck.htm.

Chapter 6: Basics of Credit

1. Jathon Sapsford, "Paper Losses: As Cash Fades, America Becomes a Plastic Nation," *Wall Street Journal*, July 23, 2004.

2. Karen Cheney, "Playing the Best Cards," *Better Homes and Gardens*, August 2004, 176.

Chapter 7: Who Stole My Identity?

1. Federal Trade Commission, "Identity Theft Survey Report," September 2003, http://www.ftc.gov/os/2003/09/synovatereport.pdf.

2. Federal Trade Commission, "Welcome to the Federal Trade Commission: Your National Resource for Identity Theft," http://www.consumer.gov/idtheft_old/index.html.

3. Federal Trade Commission, "Identity Theft Survey Report," September 2003, http://www.ftc.gov/os/2003/09/synovatereport.pdf.

Chapter 8: Get Debt Down

1. Suein Hwang, "New Group Swells Bankruptcy Court: the Middle-Aged," *Wall Street Journal*, August 6, 2004.

2. Federal Trade Commission, "Fiscal Fitness," Facts for Consumers, November 2003, http://www.ftc.gov/bcp/conline/pubs/credit/fiscal.htm.

3. Benjamin Franklin, *The Way to Wealth* (Bedford, MA: Applewood Books, 1986), 23.

Chapter 10: Kids' Money Management

1. T. Berry Brazelton, M.D., Family Answer Book: Parenthood, *Family Circle*, April 2, 2002, 34.

Chapter 11: Moms' Questions and Answers

1. David Owen, *The First National Bank of Dad* (New York: Simon & Schuster, 2003), 12.

acknowledgments

This book has been a long time in the making and would not have been complete without the contributions of:

My dear husband, John, whose experience and wisdom grace many of these pages and who, with caring and dedication, has helped so many families make progress toward their financial goals;

My wonderful friends at MOPS, especially Beth Lagerborg, who was driving the car when this book was first proposed and has championed it ever since;

My friend Jane Jarrell, who said I should write a book about moms' finances—now why didn't I think of that?!;

My technical advisors, Jim Tungate, Ralph Heffleman, Tim Williamson, and Jim Devine, who freely lent their professional expertise to this project;

My editors at Baker Publishing Group, Jennifer Leep and Stephanie Vink, whose fine eye for detail and sense of humor made the editing process (dare I say) a pleasure; and

The mothers who took time out of their very busy schedules to openly and honestly answer my dollars and sense questionnaire so that other moms might benefit. Thank you.

Cynthia Sumner is chairman of the board of Sumner National Bank, directs the bank's marketing, and provides bookkeeping and accounting services for a moderate-sized farming operation. She holds a degree in economics and an MBA with a concentration in finance. She was past contributing editor of the *MOMSense* magazine, published by MOPS International, and has authored five books: *Time Out for Mom . . . Ahhh Moments*; *Planes, Trains, and Automobiles . . . with Kids!*; *Mommy's Locked in the Bathroom*; *Family Vacations Made Simple*; and *Mom's Trapped in the Minivan*. Cynthia is also a founding member of the MOPS Speakers' Bureau. She and her husband, John, live in rural Illinois with their three children.

For information about speaking engagements, contact:
Speak Up Speaker Services
1614 Edison Shores Place
Port Huron, MI 48060
Phone: (888) 870-7719
Email: speakupinc@aol.com

Visit Cynthia's website at:
www.cynthiasumner.com

About MOPS

You take care of your children, Mom. Who takes care of you? MOPS International (Mothers of Preschoolers) provides mothers of preschoolers with the nurture and resources they need to be the best moms they can be.

MOPS is dedicated to the message that "mothering matters" and that moms of young children need encouragement during these critical and formative years. Chartered groups meet in more than 3,600 churches and Christian ministries throughout the United States and in 22 other countries. Each MOPS program helps mothers find friendship and acceptance, provides opportunities for women to develop and practice leadership skills in the group, and promotes spiritual growth. MOPS groups are chartered ministries of local churches and meet at a variety of times and locations: daytime, evenings, and on weekends; in churches, homes, and workplaces.

The MOPPETS program offers a loving, learning experience for children while their moms attend MOPS. Other MOPS resources include *MOMSense* magazine and radio, the MOPS International website, and books and resources available through the MOPShop.

With 14.3 million mothers of preschoolers in the United States alone, many moms can't attend a local MOPS group. These moms still need the support that MOPS International can offer! For a small registration fee, any mother of preschoolers can join the MOPS♥to♥Mom Connection and receive *MOMSense* magazine six times a year, a weekly Mom-E-Mail message of encouragement, and other valuable benefits.

Find out how MOPS International can help you become part of the MOPS♥to♥Mom Connection and/or join or start a MOPS group. Visit our website at www.MOPS.org. Phone us at 303-733-5353. Or email Info@MOPS.org. To learn how to start a MOPS group, call 1-888-910-MOPS.